GREENS 24/7

**More Than 100 Quick, Easy, and Delicious Recipes
for Eating Leafy Greens and Other Green Vegetables
at Every Meal, Every Day**

GREENS 24/7: *More Than 100 Quick, Easy, and Delicious Recipes for Eating Leafy Greens and Other Green Vegetables at Every Meal, Every Day*

Copyright © 2014 Quantum Publishing

The Experiment, LLC
220 East 23rd Street, Suite 301
New York, NY 10010-4674
www.theexperimentpublishing.com

This book contains the opinions and ideas of its author. It is intended to provide helpful and informative material on the subjects addressed in the book. It is sold with the understanding that the author and publisher are not engaged in rendering medical, health, or any other kind of personal professional services in the book. The author and publisher specifically disclaim all responsibility for any liability, loss, or risk—personal or otherwise—that is incurred as a consequence, directly or indirectly, of the use and application of any of the contents of this book.

The Experiment's books are available at special discounts when purchased in bulk for premiums and sales promotions as well as for fund-raising or educational use. For details, contact us at info@theexperimentpublishing.com.

Library of Congress Cataloging-in-Publication Data

Nadel, Jessica, author.
  Greens 24/7 : more than 100 quick, easy, and delicious recipes for eating leafy greens and other green vegetables at every meal / Jessica Nadel.
    pages cm
  Includes index.
  ISBN 978-1-61519-227-4 (pbk.) -- ISBN 978-1-61519-228-1 (ebook)
  1. Cooking (Vegetables) I. Title.

  TX801.N33 2014
  641.6'5--dc23
                            2014025067

ISBN 978-1-61519-227-4
Ebook ISBN 978-1-61519-228-1

Cover and text design by Lucy Parissi

Manufactured in China
Distributed by Workman Publishing Company, Inc.
Distributed simultaneously in Canada by Thomas Allen & Son Ltd.

First published December 2014
10 9 8 7 6 5 4 3 2 1

GREENS 24/7

**More Than 100 Quick, Easy, and Delicious Recipes
for Eating Leafy Greens and Other Green Vegetables
at Every Meal, Every Day**

JESSICA NADEL

THE EXPERIMENT

CONTENTS

INTRODUCING GREENS

THERE'S A GOOD REASON MAMA SAID TO EAT YOUR GREENS. Greens are brimming with vitamins, minerals, antioxidants, and other essential nutrients. They are full of chlorophyll, they are alkalizing, and they aid natural detoxification. They've also been shown to contribute to a decreased risk of many health issues, such as diabetes, obesity, and even cancer.

Even before I was a vegan, I didn't always eat a lot of greens. In fact, like a lot of kids, I think it's fair to say that green vegetables may well have been my least favorite kind of vegetable as I was growing up. Covered in enough of my mom's cheese sauce, I could definitely down a plate of broccoli, and I grew fond of salads at some point. Then somewhere along the way something changed. I started cooking for the first time on canoe trips I led at summer camp and quickly realized I loved it. Later, as I began to shop and cook at university, exploring the amazing farmers' markets, I started to branch out and try more greens.

My serious love of greens set in a few years later, when I first subscribed to a Community Supported Agriculture (CSA) veg delivery service. I was introduced to varieties of greens that were new to me, and I learned to get creative with them. From then on I was hooked.

With a love of preparing foods and a passion for delicious, wholesome, plant-based fare, I began to discover the world of greens. Leafy greens and many other green vegetables are not only some of the most nutritious things you could possibly eat, but they are so versatile, too. Green smoothies are a way of life once you start including them in your diet. Incredible pastas can be made from gardens overrun by zucchini, and kale . . . well, kale has earned a bit of a cult following over the past few years. Now it seems that when I snoop in other people's shopping baskets (don't tell me you don't do the same!), everyone's packing greens.

It's hard to walk by a farmers' market, produce stand, or any big grocery store these days without noticing a huge variety of green veggies—all sorts of packaged salad greens, heads of lettuce, sprouts, kale, Swiss chard, zucchini, and so many more. With an ever-growing trend toward healthy eating, greens are definitely the way to go. Yet many people only eat one, maybe two servings of them a day, relegated to a salad or a side dish.

The premise of this book is simple: it's possible to eat and, more importantly, enjoy more leafy greens and other green vegetables. Gone are the days of boring, mushy, boiled cabbage and broccoli. I will show you how to incorporate greens on a daily basis with easy-to-prepare meals your whole family will enjoy, no matter the time or occasion. Whether it be breakfast, lunch, or dinner, Sunday coffee with friends, or a family celebration, I've got you covered. In *Greens 24/7* you'll find recipes featuring old and trusted favorites such as spinach, kale, and chard, but hopefully you'll discover a love for some lesser-known green veggies, too. The recipes that follow are all vegan, very delicious, and you'll find that many of them are also gluten-free.

So whether you're looking for healthy, whole-food-based meals, delicious plant-based vegan recipes, or just trying to squeeze in as many green veggies as you can, this book will be an invaluable resource in your kitchen. Step outside your realm of comfort and into this book and see just how easy and delicious these healthy recipes can be. You really can have your beet green cake and eat it.

Greens can be enjoyed by anyone, anywhere, at any time of day—literally 24/7. So here's to good health!

Jess XO

Let's get to know the greens featured in this book. There are simply so many that I chose to focus on those most readily available, and those used in several of the recipes.

KALE

Kale really is a superfood! It is plentiful in vitamins A, C, and K, and is rich in fiber and protein. But that isn't all—it also boasts anti-inflammatory properties, is a good source of calcium, and is easy to grow yourself. With all of these super qualities, it will come as no surprise that this book contains more than its fair share of recipes that showcase this leafy green.

GREEN FACT: Gram for gram, kale contains 17 times more vitamin C than carrots.

BREAKFAST: Cherry-Kale Quencher Smoothie (page 24)

LUNCH: Kale Waldorf Salad with Avocado Astoria Dressing (page 97)

SNACK: Cool Ranch Kale Chips (page 50)

DINNER: Kale and Kabocha Enchiladas Verde (page 137)

DESSERT: Sweet Massaged Kale and Fruit Salad with Raw Chocolate Sauce (page 161)

SWISS CHARD

Chard stands out among the greens, with its colored stalks and veins, sometimes white, but often beautiful hues of pink, orange, and yellow. Swiss chard is brimming with vitamins A, C, E, and K, and is full of powerful antioxidants and phytonutrients. It is now thought that these phytonutrients play a role in detoxification and regulating blood sugar.

GREEN FACT: One cup of Swiss chard contains well over 300 percent of your daily recommended dose of vitamin K.

BREAKFAST: Hello Sunshine Smoothie (page 25)

LUNCH: Superfood Salad (page 104)

SNACK: Pesto Polenta Fries (with Chard and Cilantro Pesto) (pages 54 and 74)

DINNER: Orecchiette with Chard, Sundried Tomatoes, and Toasted Almonds (page 115)

DESSERT: Rhubarb and Chard Pie (page 169)

SPINACH

There's a good reason spinach is one of the most popular greens in the world: it's healthy, versatile, and, best of all, delicious! The leaves are either flat or look slightly ruffled, and take on a deeper color as they age. Young spinach leaves have a milder taste, and are better eaten raw than older leaves. Spinach is loaded with iron, which makes it a great source of energy.

GREEN FACT: Spinach leaves are rich in chlorophyll, an especially important chemical for healthy eyesight.

BREAKFAST: Sweet Spinach Pancakes (page 34)

LUNCH: Spinach Gomae (page 92)

SNACK: Chocolate Superfood Smoothie (page 20)

DINNER: Creamy Spinach Curry with Tofu Paneer (page 132)

DESSERT: Secret Ingredient Brownies (page 147)

ZUCCHINI

Zucchini is the most commonly used vegetable in the squash family, and it isn't hard to see why. It's tender, easy to cook, and can be used in a surprising variety of dishes. In fact, as long as you don't boil them, you can cook them almost any way you can imagine. Zucchini is extremely high in magnesium and fiber, essential ingredients for a healthy heart and bowels.

GREEN FACT: The potassium and magnesium in zucchini help to lower blood pressure.

BREAKFAST: Cinnamon-Zucchini Waffles (page 35)

LUNCH: Focaccia with Tomato and Zucchini (page 68)

SNACK: Grilled Radishes, Zucchini, and Asparagus with Herbed Mayo (page 70)

DINNER: Zucchini Noodle Bolognese (page 108)

DESSERT: Zucchini Chocolate Cake (page 158)

COLLARDS

Collards provide the most accessible calcium of the bunch due to less oxalate compounds (yes, you can get calcium in things other than cow's milk). They are also packed with vitamin K, as well as being an excellent source of vitamins A, C, manganese, and fiber. Collards contain phytonutrients called glucosinolates, which help detoxification and have anti-inflammatory benefits too.

GREEN FACT: Of all the cruciferous vegetables, collard greens have been shown to have the greatest cholesterol-lowering powers.

BREAKFAST: Scrambled Tofu with Collard Greens (page 30)

LUNCH: Raw Collard Wraps with Cashew "Cheese" (page 66)

SNACK: Kale, Collard, and Cabbage Sauerkraut (page 71)

DINNER: Collard and Quinoa "Cabbage Rolls" (page 133)

KIDS' PICK: Breakfast Burritos (page 39)

AVOCADO

Although some avoid avocados for being too high in fat, the fat they contain is good for you, much like the fats found in walnuts and flax seeds (oleic acid). They're high in fiber, as well as vitamins K, B6, E, and C, and with a texture so rich and creamy I just want to spread them on everything. I know what you're thinking—avocados are technically a fruit—but since they're not sweet, we're calling them a veggie here.

GREEN FACT: Eating avocado alongside foods high in beta-carotene can help increase the absorption of this antioxidant by up to 400 percent.

BREAKFAST: Breakfast Sandwich with Avocado and Arugula (page 43)

LUNCH: Raw Summer Soup (page 86)

SNACK: Mango, Avocado, and Cucumber Summer Rolls (page 58)

DINNER: Deconstructed Sushi Bowl (page 128)

DESSERT: Chocolate Hazelnut Avocado Torte (page 148)

BROCCOLI

Broccoli is an excellent source of vitamins K, C, chromium, and folate. It's also high in dietary fiber and has serious detox capabilities. Include this awesome green vegetable in your diet once or twice a week to reap these and its many other health benefits. Plus they look like tiny little trees—how cute is that!

GREEN FACT: Broccoli is particularly rich in the flavonoid kaempferol, which is thought to help offset the inflammation associated with some allergens.

BREAKFAST: Broccoli and Greens "Quiche" (page 44)

LUNCH: White Bean and Three-Green Soup (page 87)

SNACK: Mediterranean Broccoli and Barley Salad (page 101)

DINNER: Chard, Cilantro, and Cashew "Cheese" Pizza (page 118)

KIDS' PICK: Raw broccoli "trees" dipped in Arugula and White Bean Hummus (page 52)

BEET GREENS

Jackpot! If you buy a beautiful bunch of beets with the greens still on, you get a 2-for-1 vegetable deal. Eat those greens—they're amazingly healthy. They have a slightly earthy and sweet flavor, much like their roots, and can be enjoyed raw or cooked. They also have a high concentration of lutein and a higher iron content than spinach.

GREEN FACT: One cup of raw beet greens contains as much as 275 mg of lutein, important for healthy vision.

BREAKFAST: Berry and Beet Green Smoothie (page 22)

LUNCH: Beet Greens, Pear, and Maple Walnut Salad (page 93)

SNACK: Slice of Broccoli and Greens "Quiche" (page 44)

DINNER: Sweet Potato and Greens Burger (page 130)

DESSERT: Triple Chocolate Beet Greens Cake (page 157)

THE OTHER GREENS

So many greens and so little time?! The following are some of the other noteworthy greens mentioned in this book.

ARUGULA Also known as rocket, arugula is one of my favorite tender greens. It has a peppery bite and is wonderful in salads, sandwiches, and, my favorite, on pizzas. A member of the brassica family (see kale, cabbage, collards).

ASIAN GREENS If you live anywhere close to a big city, you're bound to be able to find a variety of Asian greens available. Take a chance and try a few out—there are sturdy bunches of greens that lean towards bitter (Chinese broccoli, Chinese mustard), tender leaves perfect for salads or sautés (mizuna, tatsoi), and squash, long beans, etc. Bok choy still tends to be the most common Asian green that is easily available at any grocery store, so it is the one used most frequently in this book.

ASPARAGUS Aside from being an excellent source of vitamin K, copper, and folate, asparagus also contains the prebiotic inulin, which is important to digestive health. It has also been shown to have anti-inflammatory properties. Wonderful roasted, grilled, in risotto, or even shaved raw in a salad.

BOK CHOY As noted in the Asian Greens entry above, bok choy is the most well-known Asian green in North American kitchens. It has a mild flavor with tender leaves and crunchy stalks, making it a delicious addition to both cooked and raw dishes. It is an excellent source of vitamins A, C, K, as well as of folate and calcium. A 2-cup serving of bok choy contains almost 15 percent of the daily recommended dose of calcium.

BRUSSELS SPROUTS Brussels sprouts have been shown to reduce the risks associated with multiple cancers. They can also aid in lowering cholesterol and in inflammation-related diseases such as Crohn's, irritable bowel syndrome, and arthritis. Packed with vitamins K, C, and folate. Great in soups, but also delicious shredded and eaten raw in salads. Or try roasting with olive oil and sea salt.

CABBAGE With multiple varieties available—red, green, Savoy, napa—it's hard to go wrong with cabbage. To maximize nutrition, cabbage is best eaten raw or lightly cooked (steamed or sautéed). It is an excellent source of vitamins K, C, and B6.

CELERY That unsuspecting veggie on the dip tray contains a wealth of phytonutrients that are shown to be helpful in aiding inflammatory conditions, especially inflammation of the digestive tract. Plus it's super crunchy and hydrating. It's also high in vitamin K, which aids in bloodclotting. Try it in your next smoothie!

CHAYOTE Also known as cho-cho, this squash looks a lot like a pear and is common to Mexican and Jamaican cuisines. It is high in dietary fiber, vitamin C, and folate, as well as being high in potassium and low in sodium. Best lightly steamed.

CILANTRO Cilantro has an amazing bright flavor that lends itself well to many cuisines, including Mexican, Thai, and Indian. It contains many phytonutrients and is a good source of minerals such as copper, iron, magnesium, and manganese.

CUCUMBER Vitamin C, beta-carotene, manganese, and a high water content make cucumber a hydrating, refreshing veg.

DANDELION Dandelion is the bane of many a gardener, but it is the detox darling of the greens. With its high levels of vitamins A, K, and calcium (a

1-cup serving has 10 percent of the recommended daily dose of calcium), it is also said to help cleanse the liver. If the leaves are young enough you can try them raw in salads, but more mature leaves will be strong and bitter and should be steamed or sautéed.

GREEN BEANS A good source of fiber, folate, and vitamin B2, and even a small amount of omega-3s.

NORI A good natural source of iodine (essential for thyroid function), vitamin C, and a rare plant source of vitamin B12. Sea vegetables are so many in number, they could almost have their own book!

OTHER SALAD GREENS AND LETTUCES There are so many varieties of lettuce and salad greens and they all have wonderful flavors, textures, and, of course, nutritional values. Fresh lettuce is best, so feel free to use different salad greens for recipes in this book based on what is fresh and local.

PARSLEY Poor parsley is still often relegated to a plate-side garnish, but it deserves much more attention than that given its high levels of vitamins K, C, A, folate, and iron. It's a perky addition to soups, salads, and even smoothies.

PEAS, SNOW PEAS, SUGAR SNAP PEAS Although veggies, they're also legumes (along with lentils, chickpeas, etc.) because they grow in pods. Among other standout points of nutrition, 1 cup of green peas contains a whopping 7½ g of fiber!

RADISH GREENS Super rich in calcium (a 3 oz serving has 200 mg—that's 20 percent of the recommended daily dose), and more vitamin C and protein than the radish roots we normally eat. Their flavor is actually pretty mild, so try them in a salad or your next stir-fry or sauté.

RAPINI Rapini is a little bitter, but don't be put off. Just give it a quick blanch and you're good to go. It's a staple in the Italian kitchen.

ROMAINE LETTUCE An excellent source of folate and vitamins A and K. Bring on the Caesar salads!

SAGE Sage has a history of medicinal uses and even today is still known to be useful in the treatment of inflammatory ailments and diseases.

SPIRULINA A type of blue-green algae that is a good source of protein (about 6 g per tablespoon), and contains chlorophyll. Most commonly found in powdered form at the health food store.

SUNFLOWER SPROUTS Full of folate, B vitamins, and chlorophyll—amazing for our bodily functions.

TURNIP GREENS A 2-for-1 veggie. Don't throw away the tops from that bunch of turnips—some say they're bitter, and they've certainly got a little bite, but with such a high calcium content it's hard to argue against eating them. One serving also has almost half the daily recommended dose of folate.

WATERCRESS Another brassica member, containing iron, calcium, iodine, and folate. A little peppery, but pleasingly so.

THE OTHER INGREDIENTS

You may not be familiar with some of the ingredients used in these recipes, but they're my favorites for good reason. Here's a quick run-down.

CHIA SEEDS These tiny seeds are nutrient powerhouses, full of protein, fiber, calcium, and heart-healthy omega fats. They are also able to absorb up to 10 times their weight in water, so they can be used as a thickening agent for smoothies or even as an egg substitute. Readily available at grocery stores and health food stores.

KELP NOODLES Kelp noodles are exactly that: noodles made from sea kelp. They have an interesting texture that is both crunchy and a little chewy, and they really don't have much of a taste but are a wonderful vessel for carrying the flavors of yummy vegetables and dressings. Often found in health food stores, Asian markets, or online. They are a good source of iodine and calcium and are naturally gluten-free.

MISO Fermented soybean paste. Some are stronger than others—my personal favorite is the mild, white miso paste.

NUTRITIONAL YEAST Not to be confused with baker's yeast or brewing yeast, nutritional yeast flakes have a nice "cheesy" flavor and are a great addition to sauces, gravies, or sprinkled on popcorn. Some brands are also fortified with vitamin B12, so I try to use one of those. Readily available at grocery stores and health food stores.

SHELLED HEMP SEEDS Shelled hemp seeds (also sold as hemp hearts) are small white and green seeds that are soft and delicious. They are quite plentiful in omega-3s and lovely sprinkled on yogurt, soup, and salads. Readily available at grocery stores and health food stores.

TAMARI Tamari is my preferred type of soy sauce. I find it has a smoother flavor and is salty. It has been fermented with less wheat (or in the case of gluten-free tamari, no wheat). Regular soy sauce can be substituted if tamari is unavailable. Readily available at grocery stores and health food stores.

TEMPEH Also made from soybeans, tempeh is the result of pressing the whole beans into cakes and fermenting them. It has a much stronger flavor than tofu but is just as delicious. Most often found in health food stores and larger grocery stores.

TOFU Made from soybean curd, tofu is high in protein, low in fat, and extremely versatile. Due to its overproduction for use as a livestock crop, most soy has been genetically modified, so it's best to seek out an organic, non-genetically modified option. Readily available at grocery stores and health food stores.

UMEBOSHI VINEGAR Also known as ume plum vinegar, it is the brine left over from pickling Japanese ume plums with shiso leaf, and it is tangy and quite salty and very umami. The flavor is amazing, but a little goes a long way. Most often found in health food stores.

UNREFINED CANE SUGAR Sometimes called organic cane sugar or evaporated cane juice, this is granulated sugar before the refining process. It still has its molasses in it, so it has a greater depth of flavor and is also vegan as it hasn't been filtered through bone char. Granulated sugar can be substituted if unrefined is unavailable. Readily available at grocery stores and health food stores.

5 STEPS TO GET YOUR GREEN ON

1 GO LOCAL Visit a farmers' market or a pick-your-own farm, sign up for a CSA share, or use an organic veg delivery service.

2 GROW YOUR OWN It doesn't get much easier than picking fresh greens from your own backyard. Get some seeds or seedlings and try your green thumb on for size. If in doubt, choose something easy to grow first—kale or zucchini.

3 GET YOUR RECIPE ON You're already reading this book (hurray!), so choose three recipes you want to try, make a list of things you need, go shopping, and get cracking.

4 GREEN SMOOTHIES Try a green smoothie. Yes, they have vegetables in them, but no, they don't taste like grass. On my honor.

5 CHANGE IT UP Variety is not only the spice of life, but by varying your greens you can be sure that you'll maximize your vitamin and nutrient intake. So set a goal of incorporating two new greens in your weekly meal rotation, and then change it up every few weeks.

A NOTE ABOUT THE RECIPES

All the recipes contained in this book are vegan—that means they are void of all animal products, including meat, dairy, and eggs. My family eats a plant-based diet and so all of my recipes are of course plant-based, too. We are vegan for the animals—it is the compassionate choice we make. But we also love eating this way, and our diet is rich in wholesome delicious foods, such as those found in this book. The fact that they are vegan makes them perfect for everyone around the table, vegetarians and omnivores alike. You will also find that there are many gluten-free recipes, and most contain an easy gluten-free option as well.

NUTRITIONAL INFORMATION AND HEALTHY FATS

I have to be honest—I am not one of those people who pays attention to the calories and fat in foods. I always look for the protein and fiber content, but for the most part when you are cooking your own foods made from whole food ingredients, you can trust you are eating something healthy. That being said, I do understand that many of you will want and appreciate caloric information, so there is a small table included with every recipe. You will notice that some of the recipes are high in calories and fats—these recipes include nutritious whole foods such as avocado, raw nuts, coconut milk, and seeds. Although these ingredients are high in fats, they are healthy fats that your body needs to perform various important functions, and ones that will make your skin, hair, and nails glow.

"TYPICAL DAY" GREENS MEAL PLANS

Wondering how to put it all together? Here are a few sample daily meal plans showing you how to eat your greens throughout the day.

FOR THE PARENT TRYING TO FEED THEIR KIDS GREENS

BREAKFAST: Sweet Spinach Pancakes (page 34)

LUNCH: Mango, Avocado, and Cucumber Summer Rolls (page 58)

SNACK: Chocolate-dipped Kale Chips (page 146)

DINNER: Chard, Cilantro, and Cashew "Cheese" Pizza (page 118)

DESSERT: Zucchini Oatmeal Cookies (page 151)

FOR THE SUPER BUSY, NO-TIME-TO-SLAVE-OVER-A-MEAL COOK

BREAKFAST: Berry and Beet Green Smoothie (page 22)

LUNCH: Lemony Miso Soup with Chinese Broccoli (page 83)

SNACK: Arugula and White Bean Hummus (page 52)

DINNER: Spicy Peanut Noodle Bowl (page 111)

DESSERT: Zucchini Chocolate Cake (page 158)

BREAKFAST: Scrambled Tofu with Collard Greens (page 30)

LUNCH: Superfood Salad (page 104)

SNACK: Raw Collard Wraps with Cashew "Cheese" (page 66)

DINNER: Stuffed Baked Sweet Potatoes with Broccoli, Swiss Chard, and Hummus (page 123)

DESSERT: Chocolate Avocado Pops (page 165)

BREAKFAST: Cinnamon-Zucchini Waffles (page 35)

LUNCH: Zaru Soba with Cucumber and Green Onion (page 65)

SNACK: Pesto Polenta Fries with Spicy Aïoli (page 54)

DINNER: Orecchiette with Chard, Sundried Tomatoes, and Toasted Almonds (page 115)

DESSERT: Lemon and Parsley Olive Oil Cake (page 156)

SMOOTHIES AND BREAKFASTS

TROPICAL GREEN SMOOTHIE

 Serves 2 / gluten-free

Wake up to the taste of the tropics with this super easy and very healthful breakfast. If you are new to green smoothies, this is a great starting point as spinach has one of the milder taste profiles of the greens and doesn't overpower the flavor of the fruit.

Prep: 5 mins

1 banana
½ cup (75 g) frozen mango chunks
2 cups (60 g) baby spinach
½ cup (125 ml) pineapple juice
½ cup (125 ml) water

1 Place all the ingredients in a blender and blend until incorporated and smooth. Pour into glasses and serve.

2 Garnish with a couple of chunks of frozen mango if you wish.

CALORIES (PER SERVING)	119
PROTEIN	1.9 g
TOTAL FAT	0.3 g
SATURATED FAT	0 g
CARBOHYDRATES	28.9 g
DIETARY FIBER	3.2 g
SUGARS	19 g
VITAMINS	A, B6, C, K

CHOCOLATE SUPERFOOD SMOOTHIE

 Serves 2 / gluten-free

Start your morning with chocolate! This satisfying smoothie really hits the spot when you find you've gotten out of bed on the wrong side. Full of spinach and other superfoods, such as chia seeds and maca root, your day is guaranteed to get better after sipping on this.

Prep: 5 mins

2 cups (60 g) baby spinach
1 frozen banana
1 cup (250 ml) almond milk
2 tablespoons cocoa powder or raw cacao powder
1 tablespoon chia seeds
1 tablespoon maca root powder
½ teaspoon cinnamon
1 tablespoon raw cacao nibs

1 Combine all the ingredients except for the cacao nibs in a blender and blend until smooth. Stop and scrape down the sides if necessary, and add a little extra milk as required. Blend again.

2 Pour into glasses, top with the cacao nibs, and serve.

CALORIES (PER SERVING)	158
PROTEIN	5.4 g
TOTAL FAT	6.9 g
SATURATED FAT	2.6 g
CARBOHYDRATES	23.0 g
DIETARY FIBER	8.4 g
SUGARS	7.7 g
VITAMINS	A, E, K

BERRY AND BEET GREEN SMOOTHIE

 Serves 2 / gluten-free

Beet greens tend to have a strong, earthy flavor, so this smoothie is best when young, tender greens are used. Packed with berries, it's sure to become a household favorite, especially with little ones.

Prep: 5 mins

1 cup (40 g) beet greens
1 banana
1 cup (140 g) mixed frozen berries
½ cup (75 g) strawberries
1 cup (250 ml) non-dairy milk (of choice)
3–4 ice cubes (optional)

1 Wash the beet greens and trim to 2-inch (5-cm) pieces.

2 Combine all the ingredients in a blender and blend until smooth. Pour into glasses and serve immediately.

CALORIES (PER SERVING)	129
PROTEIN	2.3 g
TOTAL FAT	2.1 g
SATURATED FAT	0 g
CARBOHYDRATES	26.7 g
DIETARY FIBER	6.2 g
SUGARS	14.4 g
VITAMINS	A, C

LEMON, GINGER, AND PARSLEY SMOOTHIE

Serves 2 / gluten-free

Feel like you're coming down with something? This smoothie is great for keeping colds at bay, and it's a real zinger, with lots of tangy lemon, spicy ginger—and parsley, too. One sip and you'll see that parsley is a refreshing addition to smoothies.

Prep: 5 mins

1 orange
½ English cucumber
1 tablespoon minced fresh ginger
1 cup (250 ml) pineapple juice
½ cup (15 g) fresh parsley leaves
juice of ½ lemon
3–4 ice cubes (optional)

1 Peel the orange and divide into segments, then chop the cucumber into chunks.

2 Place all the ingredients in a blender and blend until smooth. Pour into glasses and serve immediately, garnished with a parsley leaf if you'd like.

CALORIES (PER SERVING)	137
PROTEIN	2.3 g
TOTAL FAT	0.7 g
SATURATED FAT	0 g
CARBOHYDRATES	32.4 g
DIETARY FIBER	3.5 g
SUGARS	21.6 g
VITAMINS	A, B6, C

CHERRY-KALE QUENCHER SMOOTHIE

 Serves 2 / gluten-free

The addition of avocado to smoothies makes them really rich and creamy. This one is for my mama who is allergic to raw bananas—finally a smoothie I can share with you!

Prep: 5 mins

3 stalks kale, woody stems removed

1½ cups (375 ml) coconut water

1 cup (225 g) pitted cherries, either fresh or frozen

½ avocado

¼ cup (60 ml) pomegranate juice

1 tablespoon shelled hemp seeds

3 ice cubes (optional)

1 pitted medjool date (optional)

1. Cut or tear the kale into bite-sized pieces. Place in a blender with the coconut water and blend to give the greens a headstart in being pulverized.

2. Add the remaining ingredients and blend until smooth. Pour into glasses and serve immediately.

CALORIES (PER SERVING)	251
PROTEIN	6.7 g
TOTAL FAT	5.8 g
SATURATED FAT	1.1 g
CARBOHYDRATES	48.7 g
DIETARY FIBER	8.1 g
SUGARS	35.5 g
VITAMINS	A, C, K

BACK TO BASICS GREEN SMOOTHIE

 Serves 2 / gluten-free

Nothing fancy, no tricks up its sleeves—just a simple green smoothie to ground you and remind you why it pays to start your day this way.

Prep: 5 mins

1 banana

1 cup (150 g) strawberries

2 cups (60 g) spinach

1 cup (250 ml) non-dairy milk (of choice)

3–4 ice cubes

1. Place all the ingredients in a blender and blend until smooth. Pour into glasses and serve immediately.

CALORIES (PER SERVING)	103
PROTEIN	2.4 g
TOTAL FAT	2.1 g
SATURATED FAT	0 g
CARBOHYDRATES	21.3 g
DIETARY FIBER	4.4 g
SUGARS	11.3 g
VITAMINS	A, C

PEACHY KEEN GREEN SMOOTHIE

 Serves 2 / gluten-free

For those days when you need that extra oomph, this smoothie will fill you up with juicy sweet peaches, hydrating romaine lettuce, and a little extra energy kick from the maca powder, an ancient Incan superfood.

Prep: 5 mins

2 fresh peaches
2 stalks of celery
2 cups (90 g) romaine lettuce
1 frozen banana
1 pitted medjool date
1 cup (250 ml) almond milk
⅓ cup (85 ml) apricot juice
1 teaspoon maca root powder
(*See image, page 26, right*)

1 Wash and pit the peaches.

2 Chop the celery into large chunks and place in a blender with the romaine lettuce, banana, date, and almond milk. Blend until smooth.

3 Add the peaches, apricot juice, and maca root powder and blend again. Pour into glasses and serve with a celery leaf garnish, if desired.

CALORIES (PER SERVING)	172
PROTEIN	2.9 g
TOTAL FAT	2.1 g
SATURATED FAT	0 g
CARBOHYDRATES	37.3 g
DIETARY FIBER	5.2 g
SUGARS	27 g
VITAMINS	C

HELLO SUNSHINE SMOOTHIE

 Serves 2 / gluten-free

Sweet, refreshing, and crisp, this blend of apple, cucumber, kiwi, and chard is guaranteed to make you greet everyone you see with a smile.

Prep: 5 mins

1 sweet apple (e.g. Gala, Fuji)
1 kiwi
½ English cucumber
½ banana
1 cup (35 g) Swiss chard leaves
1 cup (250 ml) coconut water
3–4 ice cubes
(*See image, page 26, center*)

1 Peel, core, and quarter the apple. Peel the kiwi.

2 Place all the ingredients in a blender and blend until smooth. Pour into glasses and serve immediately with a slice of kiwi to garnish.

CALORIES (PER SERVING)	103
PROTEIN	1.1 g
TOTAL FAT	0.4 g
SATURATED FAT	0 g
CARBOHYDRATES	21.6 g
DIETARY FIBER	4.1 g
SUGARS	17.6 g
VITAMINS	A, B6, C

GREEN JUICE WITHOUT A JUICER

Serves 1 / gluten-free

You don't need an expensive juicer to reap the benefits of fresh green juice. Provided you have a blender and a nut milk bag (or even a good piece of cheesecloth), you can make your own green juice concoctions. Here's a favorite of mine to get you started.

Prep: 7 mins

2 cups (60 g) spinach
2 apples
1 cucumber
1-inch (2.5-cm)= piece of fresh ginger
1 cup (250 ml) water
a few drops of liquid stevia (optional)
(See image below, left)

1 Place all the ingredients in a blender and blend until smooth. Strain through the nut milk bag or cheesecloth and serve. If desired, garnish with a cucumber slice.

CALORIES (PER SERVING)	225
PROTEIN	5.8 g
TOTAL FAT	0.7 g
SATURATED FAT	0 g
CARBOHYDRATES	58.4 g
DIETARY FIBER	13.1 g
SUGARS	37.3 g
VITAMINS	A, B6, C, K

GREEN GODDESS GRANOLA

Serves 6 / gluten-free option

Making your own granola is so easy and the results are delicious. Spirulina is technically algae, but seeing as it is green and boasts many nutritional benefits, it is what makes this granola truly green. For a gluten-free option, use gluten-free oats.

Prep: 5 mins | Cook: 20 mins

1½ cups (135 g) rolled oats

¾ cup (120 g) buckwheat groats (not kasha)

¼ cup (35 g) pumpkin seeds

¼ cup (35 g) shelled hemp seeds

¼ cup (30 g) dried cranberries

2 tablespoons spirulina

¼ cup (3 or 4) medjool dates, pitted and soaked in ½ cup (125 ml) water

4 tablespoons maple syrup

raspberries, to serve

(See image, page 29, rear)

1 Preheat the oven to 300°F (150°C). Line a baking sheet with parchment paper.

2 Combine the oats, buckwheat, pumpkin seeds, hemp seeds, cranberries, and spirulina together in a large mixing bowl.

3 Drain the dates, reserving 4 tablespoons of soaking water, and place in a food processor with the maple syrup and reserved water. Blend until smooth. Pour this into the mixing bowl and stir to coat everything.

4 Spread the mixture out in a single layer on the prepared baking sheet and bake for 20 minutes, stirring halfway through, until evenly and lightly browned. Remove from the oven, leave to cool, and then break up into clusters. The granola can be stored in an airtight container for up to two weeks. Serve with fresh raspberries if you'd like.

CALORIES (PER SERVING)	280
PROTEIN	13.7 g
TOTAL FAT	7.6 g
SATURATED FAT	1.1 g
CARBOHYDRATES	40.9 g
DIETARY FIBER	4.7 g
SUGARS	13.6 g
VITAMINS	A

GREEN SMOOTHIE GRANOLA BOWLS

 Serves 2 / gluten-free option

A beautiful way to start the day. Trade in the usual glass for a bowl and dress things up with fresh berries, coconut, and show-stopping Green Goddess Granola to turn your breakfast into an edible work of art. For a gluten-free option, use gluten-free oats when making your granola.

Prep: 7 mins

1 cup (70 g) kale, woody stems removed

1 cup (30 g) spinach

1 banana

1 cup (150 g) fresh or frozen mango chunks

1 tablespoon chia seeds

1 cup (250 ml) non-dairy milk (of choice)

1 cup (100 g) Green Goddess Granola (page 27)

1 cup (125 g) fresh raspberries

2 tablespoons unsweetened coconut shreds

2 tablespoons goji berries

1 Cut or tear the kale into bite-sized pieces. Place the kale, spinach, banana, mango, chia seeds, and milk in a blender and blend until smooth.

2 Divide the smoothie between two bowls and top each with ½ cup (50 g) of granola.

3 Divide the raspberries, coconut shreds, and goji berries between the bowls and serve.

CALORIES (PER SERVING)	440
PROTEIN	19.4 g
TOTAL FAT	16.5 g
SATURATED FAT	9.2 g
CARBOHYDRATES	67 g
DIETARY FIBER	14.9 g
SUGARS	38.1 g
VITAMINS	A, C, K

SCRAMBLED TOFU WITH COLLARD GREENS

 Serves 4 / gluten-free

Nothing says brunch like a big serving of tofu scramble, complete with greens. For a true diner-style feast, roast up some mini potatoes, add a few slices of multigrain toast, and serve with a bottomless cup of coffee. If you have black salt in your spice collection, a little bit will lend an eggy flavor to the tofu.

Prep: 10 mins | **Cook**: 15 mins

1 x 16 oz (454 g) pack firm or extra-firm tofu

2 cups (70 g) collard green leaves

2 tablespoons olive oil

½ cup (75 g) red onion, diced

⅓ cup green olives, sliced

1 teaspoon turmeric

2 teaspoons gluten-free tamari

sea salt and freshly ground black pepper

1 Remove the tofu from its packaging and drain. Wrap the tofu in a clean kitchen towel and gently press the water out of it, either by hand or by placing it between two plates and weighing it down with a cast-iron pan or a few books.

2 Wash and remove the tough stems from the collards. Stack the leaves and chop into bite-sized pieces. Set aside.

3 Heat the olive oil in a large skillet pan and sauté the onions over medium-high heat until softened but not browned. Crumble the tofu into the pan and stir with the onions, coating it in oil. Add the olives, sprinkle with turmeric, and continue to cook for 5 to 7 minutes. Add more oil if needed (the tofu soaks up a lot) and season to taste with salt and pepper.

4 Move the tofu to one side of the pan and place the collards on the hot skillet. Drizzle with the tamari and sauté until wilted, about 5 minutes. Stir everything together to incorporate and serve hot with a side of toast and a garnish of lemon wedges.

CALORIES (PER SERVING)	157
PROTEIN	10.2 g
TOTAL FAT	11.9 g
SATURATED FAT	2 g
CARBOHYDRATES	5.2 g
DIETARY FIBER	2.2 g
SUGARS	1.6 g
VITAMINS	A, B6, K

AVOCADO TOAST WITH COCONUT "BACON"

Serves 4 / gluten-free option

I could eat this for breakfast every day. Actually, I think I did just that for about a month after I cooked my first batch of coconut "bacon." If you haven't tried coconut bacon yet, you're in for a treat. For a gluten-free option, use gluten-free bread.

Prep: 5 mins | Cook: 30 mins

8 slices multigrain bread
2 ripe avocados

FOR THE COCONUT "BACON"

2½ tablespoons gluten-free tamari
2 tablespoons maple syrup
1 tablespoon sesame oil
½ tablespoon liquid smoke
4 cups (300 g) unsweetened flaked coconut
pinch of sea salt

1 Preheat the oven to 325°F (160°C).

2 For the coconut "bacon," place the tamari, maple syrup, sesame oil, and liquid smoke into a large bowl and whisk to combine. Add the coconut flakes and fold them in to coat them in the mixture.

3 Spread the coconut onto a parchment-lined baking sheet and place in the oven for 20 to 30 minutes, stopping every 10 minutes to stir the coconut and rotate the pan. Once cooked, remove from the oven, sprinkle with a pinch of sea salt, and allow to cool.

4 Toast the bread and mash the avocado with a fork. Spread the avocado over the toast, top each piece with coconut bacon, and serve. Any leftover bacon will keep for one month stored in an airtight container.

CALORIES (PER SERVING)	517
PROTEIN	10.8 g
TOTAL FAT	36.9 g
SATURATED FAT	16.6 g
CARBOHYDRATES	40.9 g
DIETARY FIBER	14.2 g
SUGARS	9.3 g
VITAMINS	B6

SWEET SPINACH PANCAKES

Serves 2–3 / gluten-free option

These pancakes are actually green and totally yummy—perfect for piling up high and then drowning in maple syrup. For a gluten-free option, replace the whole wheat flour with your preferred gluten-free blend.

Prep: 5 mins | Cook: 10 mins

1 cup (125 g) whole wheat flour
1 tablespoon baking powder
pinch of salt
1 tablespoon brown sugar
½ teaspoon cinnamon
½ cup (125 ml) almond milk
1 cup (30 g) spinach
1 banana
maple syrup and fresh berries,
to serve
(*See image below, rear*)

1 Mix the flour, baking powder, salt, sugar, and cinnamon together in a large bowl. Set aside.

2 Combine the remaining ingredients in a food processor or blender and process until smooth. Add this blended mixture to the dry ingredients and stir gently to combine. If the mixture seems too thick, add a little more milk, a tablespoon at a time, until the batter is smooth and easily poured.

3 Heat a lightly oiled griddle or large frying pan. Pour the batter onto the hot griddle ¼ cup (60 ml) at a time, leaving room between the pancakes. Cook until small bubbles appear in the center of the pancakes, then flip and continue cooking, about 5 minutes per side, until golden in color. Serve warm with maple syrup and fresh berries.

CALORIES (PER SERVING)	358
PROTEIN	7.1 g
TOTAL FAT	12 g
SATURATED FAT	10.3 g
CARBOHYDRATES	58.7 g
DIETARY FIBER	4.4 g
SUGARS	10.9 g
VITAMINS	A

CINNAMON-ZUCCHINI WAFFLES

 Serves 2

These waffles will make your house smell of warming cinnamon all day
and will make your tummy sing.

Prep: 10 mins | Cook: 8 mins

¾ cup (190 ml) coconut yogurt
⅔ cup (80 g) grated zucchini
1 tablespoon coconut oil,
melted
1 tablespoon maple syrup
¾ cup (95 g) whole wheat flour
½ cup (45 g) quick-cook oats
1 tablespoon baking powder
1 teaspoon cinnamon
maple syrup and fresh berries,
to serve

(See image, page 34, front)

1 Preheat a waffle iron, if you have one.

2 In a bowl, mix together the yogurt, zucchini, oil, and maple
syrup. In a separate bowl, mix together the dry ingredients.
Add the dry ingredients to the zucchini mix and stir to incorporate.
You should end up with a thick batter.

3 Cook the batter according to your specific waffle iron
directions. If you don't have a waffle iron, heat a griddle pan
over a medium heat until hot. Brush with oil and add ½ cup
(125 ml) batter to the pan. Allow to cook for 3 to 4 minutes, then
flip and cook for another 3 to 4 minutes, until golden.

4 Serve hot with maple syrup and fresh berries.

GREEN TIP: This recipe can easily be doubled to feed more. Any
leftover waffles can be wrapped individually and refrigerated or
frozen; to reheat, simply pop in the toaster.

CALORIES (PER SERVING)	391
PROTEIN	9.9 g
TOTAL FAT	10.5 g
SATURATED FAT	7.2 g
CARBOHYDRATES	67.7 g
DIETARY FIBER	4.5 g
SUGARS	12.1 g
VITAMINS	C

KALE AND HERB CORNBREAD MUFFINS

Makes 10 / gluten-free option

These savory muffins are versatile enough to be eaten as a breakfast on their own, but you can also enjoy them alongside a tofu scramble, or even with a big bowl of White Bean and Three-Green Soup (page 87). For a gluten-free option, replace the all-purpose flour with your preferred gluten-free blend.

Prep 5 mins | Cook 25 mins

1 cup (250 ml) non-dairy milk (of choice)

1 tablespoon apple cider vinegar

1 cup (125 g) all-purpose flour

1 cup (150 g) cornmeal

½ teaspoon baking soda

2 teaspoons baking powder

1 teaspoon sea salt

¼ cup (60 ml) vegetable oil

⅓ cup (25 g) torn kale leaves

2 tablespoons fresh basil

2 tablespoons fresh chives

1 small chili (optional)

1 Preheat the oven to 350°F (180°C). Grease the holes of a muffin tin.

2 Mix the milk and vinegar together in a small bowl and set aside to curdle.

3 Meanwhile, mix together the flour, cornmeal, baking soda, baking powder, and salt in a bowl. Whisk the oil into the milk and then add to the dry ingredients, mixing well to blend.

4 Finely mince the kale, basil, chives, and chili, if using, and gently fold into the batter.

5 Scoop the mixture into the muffin tin and bake for about 20 to 25 minutes, or until a toothpick inserted into a muffin comes out clean.

CALORIES (PER SERVING)	200
PROTEIN	3.1 g
TOTAL FAT	11.7 g
SATURATED FAT	6.2 g
CARBOHYDRATES	22.4 g
DIETARY FIBER	2.2 g
SUGARS	0.9 g
VITAMINS	K

BREAKFAST BURRITOS

Serves 4 / gluten-free option

A great way to pack up breakfast to go. For someone who doesn't eat eggs, breakfast burritos have never been much fun, but now that I make them with tofu scramble I finally see what all the fuss is about. For a gluten-free option, use gluten-free wraps.

Prep: 10 mins | Cook: 20 mins

1 x 16 oz (454 g) pack firm or extra-firm tofu

2 cups (60 g) spinach, (140 g) kale, or (70 g) collard greens

2 tablespoons olive oil

½ cup (75 g) red onion, diced

1 green bell pepper, diced

1 teaspoon turmeric

4 x 10-inch (25-cm) tortilla wraps

½ cup (120 g) salsa

avocado slices

hot sauce (optional)

sea salt and freshly ground black pepper

1 Remove the tofu from its packaging and drain. Wrap the tofu in a clean tea towel and gently press the water out of it, either by hand or by placing it between two plates and weighing it down with a cast-iron pan or a few books.

2 Wash and remove the tough stems from whatever greens you're using. Stack the leaves and chop them into bite-sized pieces. Set aside.

3 Heat the oil in a large skillet pan and sauté the onions and green pepper over a medium-high heat until softened. Crumble the tofu into the pan and stir with the onions and peppers, coating it in oil. Sprinkle with turmeric and continue to cook for 5 to 7 minutes until the tofu begins to brown. Season to taste with salt and pepper.

4 Move the tofu to one side of the pan and place the greens on the hot skillet. Add a teaspoon of water and sauté for 2 to 3 minutes until wilted. Stir everything together to incorporate.

5 To assemble the burritos, lay a wrap flat and add ¾ cup of scramble to the bottom third. Add 2 tablespoons of salsa, a few avocado slices, and hot sauce if you like. Roll up the burrito from the bottom, tucking in the sides as you go.

CALORIES (PER SERVING)	358
PROTEIN	14.8 g
TOTAL FAT	16.8 g
SATURATED FAT	2.3 g
CARBOHYDRATES	39.5 g
DIETARY FIBER	5.2 g
SUGARS	3.9 g
VITAMINS	A, B6, C

BUBBLE AND SQUEAK

Serves 4 / gluten-free

A very British—and delicious—use of leftover mashed potatoes. And if you don't have leftovers, it's still a breeze to cook. This recipe is just the basic fry up, but don't let that hold you back. Add in any veg you've got: carrots, parsnips, Brussels sprouts, kale . . . go crazy. My favorite way to eat it is with a side of vegan sour cream.

Prep: 5 mins | Cook: 20 mins

4 cups (1 kg) mashed potatoes or 6 cups (900 g) potatoes, peeled and diced into bite-sized pieces

3 tablespoons vegan butter

3 tablespoons coconut oil or olive oil

¼ cup onion (40 g), diced

1½ cups (105 g) shredded cabbage

sea salt and freshly ground black pepper

1 If you are not using leftover mashed potatoes, bring a large pot of water to a boil and add the diced potatoes. Cook them until very tender, about 12 minutes. Then drain and return them to the pot along with the vegan butter, stirring to melt it. Mash the potatoes (a few lumps are fine).

2 Heat 1 tablespoon of the oil in a cast-iron pan and add the onion, sautéing until softened and translucent. Add the cabbage and continue cooking for 5 to 6 minutes over a medium-high heat. The cabbage should be tender and beginning to brown.

3 Empty the cabbage into the pot of mashed potatoes and mix to combine. Season to taste with salt and pepper.

4 Heat the remaining oil in the cast-iron pan and then add the potato mixture. Fry for 5 to 7 minutes, stirring often, until it starts to become golden brown and crispy. Then, with the back of a spatula, press down the mixture into the pan, creating a giant potato cake. Cook over medium heat for 10 minutes until heated through and a crust has formed on the bottom. If desired, place the pan under the broiler for a minute or two to brown the top. Slice and serve straight out of the pan.

CALORIES (PER SERVING)	328
PROTEIN	4.2 g
TOTAL FAT	18.7 g
SATURATED FAT	11.1 g
CARBOHYDRATES	37.5 g
DIETARY FIBER	6.2 g
SUGARS	3.7 g
VITAMINS	B6, C

BREAKFAST SANDWICH WITH AVOCADO AND ARUGULA

 Serves 2

For the serious breakfast eater. This is an homage to a sandwich I once had at a little spot in my hometown—a bit like a BLT, but with tempeh "bacon" and more veggies.

Prep: 20 mins | Cook: 25 mins

4 oz (110 g) tempeh
2 tablespoons tamari
1 tablespoon maple syrup
2 whole wheat English muffins
vegan mayonnaise
½ avocado, sliced
1 tomato, sliced
1 cup (20 g) arugula
½ cup (55 g) grated carrot

1 Preheat the oven to 375°F (190°C).

2 Place the tempeh in a steamer, or on a steaming rack over a pan of boiling water, and steam for 20 minutes.

3 Whisk the tamari and maple syrup together in an ovenproof dish. Slice the steamed tempeh into thin strips and add to the baking dish, turning to coat. Bake the tempeh for 20 minutes, turning halfway through. Finish by broiling it for a couple of minutes to crisp it up—but keep a close eye on it to ensure it doesn't burn.

4 Slice the muffins in half and toast them. Spread the muffins with the vegan mayonnaise and then layer up with the tempeh, avocado, tomato, arugula, and carrot.

CALORIES (PER SERVING)	434
PROTEIN	19.7 g
TOTAL FAT	20.9 g
SATURATED FAT	3.5 g
CARBOHYDRATES	49.1 g
DIETARY FIBER	9.2 g
SUGARS	14.2 g
VITAMINS	B6

BROCCOLI AND GREENS "QUICHE"

Serves 8 / gluten-free

Quiche is usually thought of as a dinner dish, but this is perfect for lazy weekend brunching. It's crustless so there's no pastry to fuss with, and everything mixes into one bowl for an easy clean up.

Prep: 10 mins | Cook: 40 mins

1 cup mixed green vegetables (kale, chard, peas, asparagus etc.), chopped
1 cup (90 g) broccoli, chopped
¼ cup (40 g) onion, diced
2 cups (180 g) chickpea flour
2 tablespoons nutritional yeast
¼ teaspoon turmeric
½ teaspoon sea salt
¼ teaspoon dried basil
¼ teaspoon dried thyme
½ teaspoon baking powder
1 cup (250 ml) water
2 cups (500 ml) vegetable broth
1 tablespoon olive oil

1 Preheat the oven to 400°F (200°C). Lightly grease a 9-inch (23-cm) pie pan.

2 Wash and prepare the vegetables and set aside.

3 In a large bowl, mix together the chickpea flour, yeast, turmeric, salt, basil, thyme, and baking powder. Whisk in the liquids until smooth. Stir in the vegetables and pour the mixture into the pie pan.

4 Bake for 40 minutes, or until the top is lightly browned and set. Serve warm from the oven, but it is just as good cold.

CALORIES (PER SERVING)	236
PROTEIN	13 g
TOTAL FAT	5.3 g
SATURATED FAT	0.7 g
CARBOHYDRATES	36 g
DIETARY FIBER	10.7 g
SUGARS	6.6 g
VITAMINS	B6

GREEN SIDES AND SMALL BITES

CUCUMBER PESTO CANAPÉS

 Serves 8-10 / gluten-free

Looks can be deceiving. Although these bite-sized nibbles look fancy, they take all of 5 minutes to make if you have pesto already made. Perfect for an afternoon garden party, or for when friends stop by.

Prep: 10 mins

1 cucumber
a handful of pea shoots
¼ cup (60 ml) Kale and Walnut
Pesto (page 74)
1 yellow bell pepper, sliced into
small pieces

1 Slice the cucumber into disks, about ¼-inch (0.5-cm) thick, and trim the pea shoots to 2-inch (5-cm) lengths.

2 Top each round with a dollop of pesto, followed by a few pea shoots and a few slices of pepper.

CALORIES (PER SERVING)	31
PROTEIN	1.2 g
TOTAL FAT	1.7 g
SATURATED FAT	0 g
CARBOHYDRATES	3.4 g
DIETARY FIBER	0.9 g
SUGARS	0.8 g
VITAMINS	A, B6, C, K

SWEET PEA CROSTINI

Serves 4–6 | gluten-free option

They may be a bit labor-intensive to shell, but it's well worth the trouble for a handful of fresh sweet peas. Younger peas have more sweetness to them, so they are ideal for enjoying raw in this spread. For a gluten-free option, select gluten-free bread or use gluten-free crackers.

Prep: 10 mins | Cook: 5 mins

1 cup (145 g) freshly shelled peas

½ cup (85 g) raw cashews

1 clove garlic

½ tablespoon extra virgin olive oil, plus extra for brushing

juice of ½ lemon

½ teaspoon sea salt

1 whole wheat baguette

chopped basil leaves, to garnish

(*See image, opposite*)

1 Place the peas and cashews in a food processor along with the garlic, olive oil, and lemon juice and process until smooth. Season to taste with the sea salt and set aside.

2 Slice the baguette and brush both sides of each slice lightly with olive oil. Heat the grill to medium, and grill for a few minutes, watching them closely so they don't burn.

3 Spoon a tablespoon of the pea mixture onto each slice, garnish with fresh basil, and serve.

GREEN TIP: If fresh peas are not in season, this recipe can also be made with frozen peas. Thaw 1 cup (145 g) frozen peas in a bowl of warm water for 5 minutes before making the spread.

CALORIES (PER SERVING)	124
PROTEIN	4.5 g
TOTAL FAT	7 g
SATURATED FAT	1.3 g
CARBOHYDRATES	11.5 g
DIETARY FIBER	2 g
SUGARS	1.5 g
VITAMINS	C

COOL RANCH KALE CHIPS

 Serves 4 / gluten-free

This is the dish to make for anyone who claims not to like the curly leafy green. After being coated in a rich and tangy dressing, the pieces are baked at a low temperature until dehydrated to a delicious chip. The recipe is enough for four to share, but I have been known to polish off the entire batch myself.

Prep: 15 mins | Cook: 60 to 80 mins

1 bunch curly kale (about 6½ cups/450 g)

⅔ cup (110 g) raw cashews, soaked for 4 to 6 hours

⅓ cup (85 ml) water

2 tablespoons apple cider vinegar

1 teaspoon garlic powder

1 teaspoon dried dill weed

1 teaspoon fine sea salt

¼ teaspoon freshly ground black pepper

2 tablespoons fresh parsley, minced

2 tablespoons fresh chives, minced

1 Preheat the oven to 225°F (110°C). Line two cookie sheets with parchment paper.

2 Wash the kale and, using a sharp knife, cut out the tough rib. Stack the leaves and cut into large chip-sized pieces. Pat dry and set aside. (Make sure the kale is really dry, otherwise you risk steaming your chips instead of crisping them up.)

3 Drain the soaking cashews. In a blender or food processor, combine them with the water, vinegar, dried spices, salt, and pepper, and blend until a thick, smooth texture is achieved. You may add more liquid a tablespoon at a time, if required.

4 Stir in the parsley and chives. Combine the cashew mixture with the kale in a large bowl and toss well so that all of the leaves are coated. Spread out the kale on the two cookie sheets, ensuring it is spread out in a single layer.

5 Bake for 60 to 80 minutes with the oven door open a crack. Gently rearrange the kale after 45 minutes of cooking time and rotate the cookie sheets to ensure even baking. Keep a close eye on them to ensure they don't burn; they should just crisp up. Remove from the oven and allow to cool before diving in.

CALORIES (PER SERVING)	192
PROTEIN	8.6 g
TOTAL FAT	11.7 g
SATURATED FAT	2.2 g
CARBOHYDRATES	18.3 g
DIETARY FIBER	5 g
SUGARS	3.9 g
VITAMINS	A, C, K

ARUGULA AND WHITE BEAN HUMMUS

Serves 8 / gluten-free

Arugula's got such a lovely bite to it that this hummus is perfectly tangy even without the addition of lemon juice. Homemade hummus is so much better than store-bought and it takes all of 5 minutes to make—in fact, I highly recommend you make this hummus immediately so that you've got something to snack on while you finish browsing through the book.

Prep: 5 mins

2 cups (360 g) cooked or canned white beans, drained and rinsed

1½ cups (30 g) packed arugula

3 tablespoons tahini

2 tablespoons olive oil

2 tablespoons water

½ teaspoon sea salt

1 Place all the ingredients in a food processor and purée until smooth. You could opt to reduce the quantity of oil and equally increase the water until the desired consistency is achieved.

CALORIES (PER SERVING)	214
PROTEIN	11.6 g
TOTAL FAT	6.9 g
SATURATED FAT	1 g
CARBOHYDRATES	28.5 g
DIETARY FIBER	7.4 g
SUGARS	1.1 g
VITAMINS	A, C, K

SALTED CUCUMBER PICKLES

 Serves 4 / gluten-free

Nothing is worse than when you've got a hankering for a burger piled high with pickles and the jar in the fridge is empty. Here's a quick recipe to fake your way through with simple cucumber pickles. Kirby cucumbers have few seeds and lots of little bumps on their skin—perfect for pickling.

Prep: 15 mins

½ teaspoon sea salt
¼ teaspoon unrefined cane sugar
⅓ cup (85 ml) rice vinegar
4 kirby cucumbers
(*See image, page 52, rear*)

1 In a bowl, combine the salt, sugar, and vinegar together and stir until the salt and sugar dissolve. (Note: If using pre-seasoned rice vinegar, omit the sugar.)

2 Trim the ends off the cucumbers and slice thinly. Add them to the vinegar and stir to coat. The vinegar will not cover them completely. Leave them to sit for 10 minutes, stirring once or twice. Store in the fridge and consume within two days.

VARIATIONS
Add a fresh sliced jalapeño
Add 1 teaspoon grated fresh ginger
Add thin slices of red onion

CALORIES (PER SERVING)	61
PROTEIN	1.7 g
TOTAL FAT	0.6 g
SATURATED FAT	0 g
CARBOHYDRATES	11.2 g
DIETARY FIBER	1.7 g
SUGARS	0 g
VITAMINS	B6, C

PESTO POLENTA FRIES WITH SPICY AÏOLI

Serves 4 | gluten-free

These polenta fries are a breeze to whip up and are a huge crowd-pleaser. You can even prepare the polenta a day in advance so that you only need to slice and bake it—just be sure to cover the baking sheet tightly with plastic wrap to keep the polenta from drying out.

Prep: 75 mins | Cook: 30 mins

3½ cups (875 ml) water
sea salt
1⅓ cups (200 g) cornmeal
¼ cup (60 ml) Kale and Walnut Pesto (page 74)
vegetable oil, for baking

FOR THE SPICY AÏOLI
½ cup (125 ml) vegan mayonnaise
1 tablespoon Sriracha chili sauce
squeeze of fresh lime juice

1 Line two baking sheets with parchment paper. Bring the water to a boil in a medium-sized pot. Add a pinch of salt and stir to dissolve, then slowly add the cornmeal, stirring constantly.

2 Reduce the heat to low. Add the pesto and continue to stir until the polenta mixture thickens significantly and pulls away from the sides of the pot. This will take anywhere from 2 to 10 minutes.

3 Scoop the polenta onto one of the prepared baking sheets and press it down to a ¾-inch (2-cm) thickness; it will be very sticky so use a silicone spatula or even wet hands. Allow the pan to sit for 1 to 2 hours to allow the polenta to set; you can pop it in the fridge to speed up the process.

4 Once set, the polenta is ready to be sliced into fries. Preheat the oven to 425°F (220°C), then slice the polenta with a sharp knife, or use a pizza cutter.

5 Transfer the fries to the second baking sheet, brush or spritz lightly with vegetable oil, and place in the oven. Bake for 20 minutes, turning the fries halfway through, until they are slightly browned and crispy on the outside.

6 Meanwhile, mix all the aïoli ingredients together in a small bowl.

7 Remove the fries from the oven, season with a little salt, and serve with the spicy aïoli for dipping.

CALORIES (PER SERVING)	349
PROTEIN	5.7 g
TOTAL FAT	17.8 g
SATURATED FAT	1.7 g
CARBOHYDRATES	42.3 g
DIETARY FIBER	5.5 g
SUGARS	0 g
VITAMINS	A

CHAYOTE CEVICHE

Serves 4 / gluten-free

Traditionally, ceviche is a South American dish of raw fish marinated in citrus and olive oil and served as an appetizer. With a little green makeover, we're using chayote squash as a stand-in. It's light and refreshing, and perfect served up with gluten-free tortilla chips and a few cold beers.

Prep: 70 mins | Cook: 3 mins

1 chayote
½ orange bell pepper, diced
¼ cup (40 g) red onion, finely diced
½ avocado, diced
½ cup (75 g) mango, diced
1 tablespoon chopped cilantro
2 tablespoons fresh lime juice
1 tablespoon orange juice
1 tablespoon olive oil
pinch of sea salt

1 Cut the chayote in half and remove the pit. Peel, dice, and blanch for 3 minutes in boiling water. Drain, then rinse in cold water to stop the cooking process.

2 In a large bowl, combine the chayote with the bell peppers, onion, avocado, mango, and cilantro.

3 Whisk together the lime juice, orange juice, oil, and salt. Pour over the ceviche and stir. Cover and leave to marinate for at least 1 hour prior to serving. If you wish, you could garnish the dish with a cilantro leaf or two.

CALORIES (PER SERVING)	139
PROTEIN	1.4 g
TOTAL FAT	8.7 g
SATURATED FAT	1.6 g
CARBOHYDRATES	15.9 g
DIETARY FIBER	4 g
SUGARS	10.1 g
VITAMINS	A, B6, C

MANGO, AVOCADO, AND CUCUMBER SUMMER ROLLS

 Serves 3 / gluten-free

Sweet, juicy mango paired with creamy avocado and cool, crisp cucumber is always a good idea. These summer rolls are perfect picnic fare.

Prep: 10 mins | Cook: 15 mins

1 small mango
½ avocado
⅓ English cucumber
6 teaspoons toasted sesame seeds
6 rice paper sheets
6 sprigs cilantro
1 cup (175 g) cooked rice noodles

FOR THE DIPPING SAUCE
2 tablespoons almond butter
2 tablespoons gluten-free tamari
juice of ½ lime
¼ teaspoon powdered ginger
pinch of fresh black pepper

1 Peel and slice the mango, avocado, and cucumber into long, thin strips and set aside with the cooked rice noodles and chopped cilantro, ready for filling.

2 Set up your working space with a clean tea towel, folded in half, and a shallow pan or pie plate with 2 inches (5-cm) hot water in the bottom.

3 Place a sheet of rice paper in the water and submerge it to soften. This will take less than a minute. Remove it gently and lay it out on the towel, being mindful not to rip it. Sprinkle a teaspoon of sesame seeds onto the paper, followed by one-sixth of each filling, centered near the bottom of the paper. Fold in each side to meet in the middle and roll it up tightly as you would a burrito, making sure all the fillings are tucked in. Repeat this process with all six sheets.

4 For the dipping sauce, whisk together all the ingredients in a small bowl. Thin with water if necessary, adding a teaspoon at a time, until the sauce is smooth and thick.

CALORIES (PER SERVING)	321
PROTEIN	7.9 g
TOTAL FAT	16.1 g
SATURATED FAT	2.4 g
CARBOHYDRATES	38.1 g
DIETARY FIBER	5.2 g
SUGARS	5.3 g
VITAMINS	B6, C

SESAME CABBAGE, CARROT, AND TEMPEH ROLLS

Serves 6 / gluten-free

This is my favorite cabbage recipe—I love it served in lettuce leaves, or rolled up in rice paper, and I've even been known to just serve it up on its own in a bowl. If tempeh is unavailable, try using extra-firm tofu instead (omit the steaming step), pressing it in a tea towel to release some of its water content. Choose a gluten-free tempeh if necessary.

Prep: 20 mins | Cook: 30 mins

4 oz (110 g) tempeh

1 head Boston or Bibb lettuce

2 tablespoons toasted sesame oil

1-inch (2.5-cm) piece fresh ginger, peeled and minced

1 head napa cabbage, shredded

3 large carrots, peeled and cut into matchsticks

2 green onions, diced

2 tablespoons tamari

1 tablespoon sesame seeds

FOR THE SESAME MISO SAUCE

2 tablespoons tahini

1 tablespoon toasted sesame oil

2 teaspoons white miso paste

½ teaspoon Sriracha or other chili sauce

water for thinning

(*See image, opposite*)

CALORIES (PER SERVING)	183
PROTEIN	8.5 g
TOTAL FAT	12. 8 g
SATURATED FAT	1.9 g
CARBOHYDRATES	12.4 g
DIETARY FIBER	3.8 g
SUGARS	4.8 g
VITAMINS	A, B6, C

1 Place the tempeh in a steamer, or on a steaming rack over a pan of boiling water, and steam for 20 minutes. Allow it to cool, then cut into small ¼-inch (0.5-cm) cubes. Set aside.

2 While the tempeh is steaming, prepare the lettuce wraps. Remove whole leaves from the head of lettuce, wash gently, and pat dry. Set these aside until the filling is prepared.

3 For the sesame miso sauce, whisk the tahini, oil, miso paste, and chili sauce together in a small dish. The resulting mixture will be thick, so add water a tablespoon at a time, until the desired consistency is reached. Set aside.

4 Heat the sesame oil with the ginger. Add the tempeh and cook over a medium-high heat until browned, about 5 to 7 minutes. Add the cabbage, carrots, and green onions and stir carefully to avoid spillage. Add the tamari, raise the heat to high, and cook while stirring for 2 to 3 minutes. The cabbage will cook down significantly and the carrots will soften but retain a little crunch. If there is still liquid in the pan, continue cooking until the pan is almost dry.

5 Spoon the mixture into the lettuce wraps, sprinkle with sesame seeds, and serve with sesame miso sauce for dipping.

GREEN TIP: If napa cabbage is unavailable, try savoy cabbage.

SAUTÉED DANDELION WITH LEMON AND PINE NUTS

 Serves 4 | gluten-free

One bite of these greens and you'll never look at those pesky garden weeds in the same way! Please don't go picking them from your neighbor's lawn or from the park, however—they may have been sprayed with chemicals. Always buy them at the grocery store, from a local farmer, or harvest them from your own organic lawn.

Prep: 5 mins | Cook: 7 mins

9 cups (450 g) dandelion greens (about 1 large bunch)
1 tablespoon olive oil
2 tablespoons lemon juice
1 teaspoon agave nectar
pinch of chili flakes
sea salt and freshly ground black pepper
⅛ cup (20 g) pine nuts, toasted
(*See image, opposite*)

1 Wash and trim the dandelion greens to 3-inch (7.5-cm) pieces, discarding the tough ends of the stems. Spin or pat dry.

2 Heat the oil in a large skillet over a medium-high heat. Add the greens and sauté them until they begin to wilt, then add the lemon juice, agave, and chili flakes. Continue to cook for another 2 minutes while stirring, until the greens are tender and cooked.

3 Season lightly with salt and pepper, transfer to a serving dish, and top with the pine nuts.

GREEN TIP: If you've never tasted dandelion greens before, their bitterness can be a little overwhelming at first. However, give yourself a chance to become accustomed to their flavor—you'll love them!

CALORIES (PER SERVING)	121
PROTEIN	3.9 g
TOTAL FAT	7.8 g
SATURATED FAT	1 g
CARBOHYDRATES	12.4 g
DIETARY FIBER	4.3 g
SUGARS	2.2 g
VITAMINS	A, B6, C, K

DANDELION COLCANNON

Serves 4-6 / gluten-free

Colcannon is a traditional Irish dish of mashed potatoes and kale. Here, it's getting a little freshening up with wild and tangy dandelion greens. If dandelion greens aren't available, mustard greens are a perfect stand-in.

Prep: 10 mins | Cook: 20 mins

6 cups (900 g) Yukon gold potatoes

3 tablespoons vegan butter

1 cup (150 g) onion, diced

3 cups (150 g) dandelion greens, chopped (discard the tough ends of the stems)

1 cup (250 ml) unsweetened soy milk

sea salt

1 Peel and chop the potatoes while bringing a large pot of salted water to a boil. Add the potatoes and cook for about 15 minutes until they are easily pierced with a fork. Drain in a colander and return the pot to the stove.

2 Add the butter to the pot and melt over a medium heat. Add the onion and dandelion greens, and sauté until wilted, about 2 minutes. Return the potatoes to the pot along with the milk and mash everything together. Season to taste with salt and serve.

CALORIES (PER SERVING)	264
PROTEIN	6.2 g
TOTAL FAT	10.1 g
SATURATED FAT	2.6 g
CARBOHYDRATES	39.6 g
DIETARY FIBER	4.3 g
SUGARS	4.4 g
VITAMINS	A, B6, C, K

PUFF PASTRY WITH FENNEL AND TURNIP GREENS

 Serves 8-10

I love puff pastry for appetizers and it's really easy to work with. This dish can be cut into bite-sized pieces for an appetizer to serve many, or pair it with a big salad for a light dinner for four people.

Prep: 5 mins | Cook: 25 mins

1 tablespoon extra virgin olive oil

½ fennel bulb, thinly sliced

2 cloves garlic, minced

¼ onion, thinly sliced

1 bunch turnip greens, chopped

flour for rolling out

1 x 14 oz (397 g) pack vegan puff pastry

sea salt and freshly ground black pepper

1 Preheat the oven to 375°F (190°C). Line a cookie sheet with parchment paper.

2 Heat the olive oil in a large skillet. Add the fennel and sauté for a few minutes until softened. Add the garlic, onion, and turnip greens. Continue to sauté until the turnip greens are tender, about 3 to 4 minutes. Season with salt and pepper and then remove from the heat.

3 Roll out the puff pastry on a floured surface to a rectangle approximately 10 x 15 inches (25 x 38-cm) and transfer to the cookie sheet. Spread out the fennel and turnip green mixture, leaving a 1-inch (2.5-cm) border around the edge for it to puff up during baking. Place in the oven and bake for 15 to 20 minutes, or until the puff pastry is flaky and just starting to brown. Remove from the oven, slice, and serve.

GREEN TIP: If turnip greens are not available, an arugula and spinach mix (about 4 loosely packed cups) makes for a delicious stand-in.

CALORIES (PER SERVING)	196
PROTEIN	3.4 g
TOTAL FAT	12 g
SATURATED FAT	5.9 g
CARBOHYDRATES	20.1 g
DIETARY FIBER	3.1 g
SUGARS	1.3 g
VITAMINS	A, B6, C, K

ZARU SOBA WITH CUCUMBER AND GREEN ONION

Serves 4 / gluten-free option

This is a dish for sharing, and communal meals are always fun! For a gluten-free option, ensure your noodles are 100% buckwheat, as many also contain wheat flour.

Prep: 20 mins | Cook: 5 mins

1 x 16 oz (454 g) pack soba noodles
½ English cucumber, cut into long, thin strips
1 red bell pepper, cut into long, thin strips
½ cup (45 g) daikon, cut into thinly sliced rounds
2 green onions, finely minced
1 tablespoon freshly grated ginger
1 tablespoon prepared wasabi
2 tablespoons sesame seeds, plus extra for sprinkling
1 sheet toasted nori, cut into thin strips

FOR THE DIPPING SAUCE
1½ cups (375 ml) boiling water
1 tablespoon white miso paste
¼ cup (60 ml) mirin
¼ cup (60 ml) tamari
1 tablespoon rice vinegar
1 teaspoon unrefined cane sugar

1 Cook the noodles according to package directions. Drain and rinse under cold water until the water runs clear. Set the noodles aside on a clean, dry tea towel to dry.

2 Place the cut vegetables in little piles on a large plate or serving platter. Arrange the green onions, ginger, wasabi, and sesame seeds in their own individual dishes.

3 For the dipping sauce, pour the boiling water into a bowl or mug. Add the miso paste and whisk to dissolve. In a small saucepan, bring the mirin, tamari, vinegar, and sugar to a boil. Once boiling, remove from the heat and stir in the miso broth.

4 To serve, plate several little bite-sized bundles of noodles onto each bamboo mat or plate. Top each with a sprinkling of nori shreds and sesame seeds. Give each guest an individual bowl of dipping sauce.

5 To eat, season the dipping sauces by adding green onion, wasabi, ginger, and sesame seeds, according to personal taste. Pick up a bite-sized bundle of noodles with chopsticks and dip them into the sauce before eating. Dip the vegetables into your sauce the same way. At the end of the meal, you could add hot water to your dipping bowl and turn what's remaining into a broth to drink up too.

CALORIES (PER SERVING)	512
PROTEIN	20.6 g
TOTAL FAT	5.2 g
SATURATED FAT	0 g
CARBOHYDRATES	96.4 g
DIETARY FIBER	8.4 g
SUGARS	11.3 g
VITAMINS	C

RAW COLLARD WRAPS WITH CASHEW "CHEESE"

 Serves 4 / gluten-free

Collard leaves are so smooth and big that they make a perfect tortilla for wrapping. These wraps are filled with fresh vegetables and a rich and creamy raw cashew "cheese," making for a perfect light bite.

Prep: 10 mins

4 large collard leaves

2 large carrots, grated

1 red or yellow bell pepper, sliced into thin strips

2 cups (170 g) sunflower sprouts or pea shoots

FOR THE CASHEW "CHEESE"

1 cup (170 g) raw cashews, soaked for 4 hours

1 tablespoon umeboshi plum vinegar

3–4 tablespoons water

freshly ground black pepper

1 For the cashew "cheese," rinse and drain the cashews. Place them in a food processor with the vinegar and 2 tablespoons of the water. Blend for 3 to 4 minutes, stopping to scrape down the sides of the bowl as you go. Add more water, a tablespoon at a time, until a smooth, thick consistency is reached, much like creamy ricotta. Season to taste with pepper.

2 Wash and dry the collards. One at a time, carefully remove the tough center stem with a paring knife. Your leaf will now be attached at the top by about 3 inches (7.5-cm).

3 To assemble, lay each collard leaf flat and overlap the two tails to close the gap. Spread a quarter of the cashew cheese about an inch (2.5-cm) from the bottom of each leaf. On top of this add a quarter of the carrots, peppers, and sprouts or shoots. Starting at the bottom, carefully roll up the collards, tucking in the edges as you go. Lay them down on the join of the roll so that they stay together. Using a serrated knife, slice in half and serve.

CALORIES (PER SERVING)	289
PROTEIN	8.7 g
TOTAL FAT	19.9 g
SATURATED FAT	3.9 g
CARBOHYDRATES	23.3 g
DIETARY FIBER	4.6 g
SUGARS	6.1 g
VITAMINS	A, B6, C, K

FOCACCIA WITH TOMATO AND ZUCCHINI

 Serves 8

Focaccia is a nice alternative to pizza, and is wonderful eaten warm and dipped in a high-quality balsamic vinegar. I love to enjoy it with a big, beautiful salad and use it to mop up my plate.

Prep: 60 mins | Cook: 15 to 18 mins

1 teaspoon granulated sugar

1 cup (250 ml) warm water

1 teaspoon active yeast

2½ cups + 2 tablespoons (330 g) all-purpose flour

1 teaspoon sea salt, plus extra for sprinkling

2 tablespoons extra virgin olive oil

½ cup (75 g) cherry tomatoes, halved

½ zucchini, thinly sliced

4 sprigs fresh thyme

(See image, page 46)

1 Begin by proofing the yeast. Stir the sugar into the warm water until dissolved, then sprinkle the yeast on top. Leave for 5 minutes, after which it should be foamy on top. If it isn't, the yeast is no longer active and you'll need to start over with fresh yeast.

2 Stir together the flour and salt. Add the proofed yeast mixture along with 1 tablespoon of olive oil and mix with a wooden spoon until a sticky dough pulls together. Turn it out onto a lightly floured surface and knead until smooth and elastic, about 5 to 7 minutes.

3 Place the dough in a lightly oiled bowl and turn it to coat with the oil. Cover with a damp tea towel and place it somewhere warm to rise for 40 minutes. It should double in size.

4 Preheat the oven to 400°F (200°C). Place the dough on an oiled baking sheet. Press the dough down with your fingers, stretching it out to a ½- to 1-inch (1 to 2.5-cm) thickness. Make divots with your fingers to trap little golden pockets of oil, then brush or drizzle with the remaining tablespoon of olive oil and top with the tomatoes (cut-side up), zucchini, thyme, and a generous sprinkling of sea salt.

5 Bake for 15 to 18 minutes, until golden. Serve warm.

CALORIES (PER SERVING)	187
PROTEIN	4.7 g
TOTAL FAT	4 g
SATURATED FAT	0.6 g
CARBOHYDRATES	32.9 g
DIETARY FIBER	1.5 g
SUGARS	1.1 g
VITAMINS	A, C, K

ISRAELI COUSCOUS WITH PEAS AND MINT

Serves 4

My brother Jamie is quite the cook, and he often creates big veggie-centric meals. He made this dish for my parents, with rave reviews, and my father insisted it be shared with the world via my cookbook. It's delicious.

Prep: 5 mins | Cook: 25 mins

2½ cups (625 ml) low-sodium vegetable broth

2 cups (360 g) Israeli couscous

1½ cups (220 g) peas, fresh or frozen and thawed

1 tablespoon chopped fresh mint

1 Bring the vegetable broth to a boil in a pot. Add the couscous, give it a quick stir, then reduce the heat to low and cover. Cook for 15 minutes.

2 When only 2 minutes of cooking time remain, remove the lid and stir in the peas. Cover again for the final 2 minutes. Remove from the heat, allow to sit for 5 minutes, then fluff with a fork, stir in the mint, and serve. You could garnish the dish with a sprig of mint if you wish.

CALORIES (PER SERVING)	379
PROTEIN	15.3 g
TOTAL FAT	0.8 g
SATURATED FAT	0 g
CARBOHYDRATES	75.6 g
DIETARY FIBER	7.2 g
SUGARS	3.1 g
VITAMINS	C

GRILLED RADISHES, ZUCCHINI, AND ASPARAGUS WITH HERBED MAYO

 Serves 4–6 / gluten-free

There's nothing better than garden-fresh vegetables grilled on the barbecue. This dish is quick and easy, and a tasty accompaniment to your next backyard dinner party. If it's too cold to eat outside, just make them indoors under a broiler.

Prep: 5 mins | Cook: 10 mins

6–8 radishes
1 zucchini
12 asparagus spears
olive oil
sea salt

FOR THE HERBED MAYO

1 cup (250 ml) vegan mayonnaise
¼ cup (10 g) fresh basil
2 sprigs fresh thyme
1 tablespoon fresh parsley
1 tablespoon fresh chives

1 Heat your barbecue grill to high. Trim the greens from the radishes, leaving an inch or two. Slice the zucchini and snap off the woody ends of the asparagus. Place the vegetables in a large dish and drizzle with oil. Toss to coat and sprinkle with salt.

2 Grill the vegetables in a grill basket with the barbecue cover open, until tender and beginning to char. You may need to cook them in two batches—if so, keep them warm on the warming shelf in the barbecue, or in an oiled baking dish covered with foil.

3 For the herbed mayo, chop the herbs and mix with the vegan mayonnaise in a small bowl. Serve alongside the veggies for dipping.

GREEN TIP: Don't toss those radish greens—throw them in your next batch of fresh pesto.

CALORIES (PER SERVING)	181
PROTEIN	1.9 g
TOTAL FAT	17 g
SATURATED FAT	0.9 g
CARBOHYDRATES	7.5 g
DIETARY FIBER	2 g
SUGARS	1.9 g
VITAMINS	C

KALE, COLLARD, AND CABBAGE SAUERKRAUT

 Serves 10 | gluten-free

Making your own sauerkraut is easy—all you need are your vegetables and salt. The trick is making sure enough water is released from the veggies during the salt massage so that once in the jar they are fully submerged. From there it's just a matter of waiting until the kraut is as tangy as you like. This kraut contains a trio of green goodness, with kale, collards, and cabbage.

Prep: 20 mins (plus 3 days inactive)

1 bunch purple kale
½ head green cabbage
2 cups (70 g) collards
1–2 teaspoons sea salt

1 Shred the greens as small as possible and place in a large bowl. Toss them with a good amount of sea salt and begin to massage. This takes a lot of arm power as you need to keep working it until the juices start releasing, and then work it some more. It may take up to 10 minutes. You want enough liquid released so that the veggies will be completely submerged when weighted down.

2 Pack the greens and juices into a glass jar or bowl (no metal) and press down. Place a second, smaller glass jar or bowl on top and weigh it down to keep the greens submerged. Cover with a cloth and sit in a warm spot for three days.

3 Check it every day to make sure it's all still covered in liquid, and to give it a taste. When you find it's tangy enough for you, you can stop the fermentation process by placing it in the fridge. If any mold has formed on top, just skim it off—it's harmless.

4 Enjoy the sauerkraut as a condiment, as a salad or sandwich topper, or straight from the jar. If the finished product is a bit too salty for your taste, rinse it gently under lukewarm water before eating.

CALORIES (PER SERVING)	33
PROTEIN	2 g
TOTAL FAT	0.1 g
SATURATED FAT	0 g
CARBOHYDRATES	7.2 g
DIETARY FIBER	1.8 g
SUGARS	1.2 g
VITAMINS	A, B6, C, K

SPICY GARLIC BOK CHOY

 Serves 4 / gluten-free

It's pretty hard to go wrong with sesame oil, fresh garlic, and a little chili heat. This recipe is definitely my go-to for super fast, get-in-my-belly greens. If you don't have bok choy, don't worry—any leafy green can stand in here. If using something a little heartier like full-sized bok choy, yu choy (Chinese greens), or Chinese broccoli, increase the covered cooking time by 3 to 4 minutes.

Prep: 5 mins | Cook: 7 mins

4 heads baby bok choy

1 tablespoon toasted sesame seeds

2 tablespoons sesame oil

2 cloves garlic

1 teaspoon Sriracha or hot chili sauce

1 tablespoon gluten-free tamari

1 Slice the bok choy in half lengthwise and rinse well. Place in a colander to drip dry, but you do want to retain a little moisture.

2 If your sesame seeds are raw, toast them in a dry skillet over medium heat for 2 to 3 minutes. Stir constantly and once they begin to brown, remove them from the heat and set aside.

3 Heat the oil over medium–high heat in a large skillet. Mince the garlic and add to the oil, stirring for a minute to avoid the garlic burning. Add the bok choy to the pan, cut-side down, to sear. Flip after 30 seconds to sear the other side.

4 Whisk together the hot sauce and tamari. Pour this over the greens, give them a quick stir, then cover and let them cook for 2 to 3 minutes. Test the bok choy by piercing the stem with a fork—if tender, they're done. Plate and sprinkle with sesame seeds, then serve.

CALORIES (PER SERVING)	189
PROTEIN	13.6 g
TOTAL FAT	9.6 g
SATURATED FAT	1.4 g
CARBOHYDRATES	19.8 g
DIETARY FIBER	8.7 g
SUGARS	9.9 g
VITAMINS	A, B6, C

KALE AND WALNUT PESTO

 Serves 4 | gluten-free

This kale and walnut pesto is especially delicious when paired with gnocchi.

Prep: 5 mins

2 cups (140 g) kale, woody stems removed
1 cup (45 g) fresh basil leaves
½ cup (50 g) raw walnuts
2 tablespoons extra virgin olive oil
2 tablespoons fresh lemon juice
2 tablespoons nutritional yeast
1 clove garlic
½ teaspoon sea salt
freshly ground black pepper

1 Place all the ingredients in a food processor and process until smooth, stopping to scrape down the sides of the bowl as necessary. Season to taste with pepper and more salt.

CALORIES (PER SERVING)	178
PROTEIN	6.8 g
TOTAL FAT	14.8 g
SATURATED FAT	1.5 g
CARBOHYDRATES	7.9 g
DIETARY FIBER	2.9 g
SUGARS	0 g
VITAMINS	A, C, K

CHARD AND CILANTRO PESTO

 Serves 4 | gluten-free

Who says pesto has to contain basil? This non-traditional chard and cilantro pesto is an amazing change from the standard fare. It's also nut-free for those with allergies.

Prep: 5 mins

2 cups (70 g) chard leaves
1 cup (45 g) fresh cilantro, leaves and stems
½ cup (70 g) raw sunflower seeds
2 tablespoons extra virgin olive oil
2 tablespoons fresh lemon juice
2 tablespoons nutritional yeast
½ teaspoon sea salt
freshly ground black pepper

1 Place all the ingredients in a food processor and process until smooth, stopping to scrape down the sides of the bowl as necessary. Season to taste with pepper and more salt.

CALORIES (PER SERVING)	119
PROTEIN	4.1 g
TOTAL FAT	10.4 g
SATURATED FAT	1.4 g
CARBOHYDRATES	4.7 g
DIETARY FIBER	2.4 g
SUGARS	0.6 g
VITAMINS	A, C, K

GREEN SOUPS AND SALADS

CREAM OF ASPARAGUS SOUP

 Serves 4 / gluten-free

I always find myself smiling when I see asparagus arriving in the grocery store because it means spring is on the way. Cream of asparagus soup is a simple way to bridge the changing of the seasons, and this non-dairy version utilizes a rich and luxurious cashew "cream."

Prep: 10 mins | Cook: 25 mins

2 tablespoons olive oil

1 leek, rinsed and chopped into 1-inch (2.5 cm) pieces

5 cups (675 g) asparagus

4 cups (1 l) vegetable broth or vegan "chicken" broth

2 tablespoons lemon juice

½ teaspoon sea salt

¼ teaspoon freshly ground black pepper

⅓ cup (55 g) raw cashews, soaked for at least 4 hours

⅓ cup (85 ml) water

2 teaspoons chopped fresh chives, to serve

(See image, opposite, front)

1 Heat the oil in a medium saucepan over medium heat. Add the leeks and cook until softened, about 10 minutes.

2 Snap the woody ends off the asparagus and chop the spears into 2-inch (5-cm) pieces. Add to the saucepan with the broth, lemon juice, and salt and pepper. Bring to a boil, then reduce heat to a simmer and cook for 10 minutes until the asparagus is tender.

3 Remove ¼ cup (50 g) of the asparagus tips and reserve. Using either a standing blender (in batches) or an immersion blender, purée the soup.

4 Drain the cashews from the soaking water. Add a fresh ⅓ cup (80 ml) of water to the cashews and blend until smooth. Add this "cream" to the soup, stir well, and return to a boil. Remove from the heat and serve in shallow bowls garnished with the reserved asparagus tips and fresh chives.

CALORIES (PER SERVING)	229
PROTEIN	11.2 g
TOTAL FAT	15.1 g
SATURATED FAT	2.8 g
CARBOHYDRATES	15.6 g
DIETARY FIBER	4.5 g
SUGARS	5.8 g
VITAMINS	A, C, K

CELERY, LENTIL, AND GREEN TOMATO WARMER

Serves 4–6 | gluten-free

I originally came up with this delicious soup in late summer when a friend presented me with a basket of green tomatoes from her farm, picked to escape a frosty fate.

Prep: 10 mins | Cook: 35 mins

2 tablespoons olive oil

1 medium onion, diced

4 ribs celery, chopped

2 cloves garlic, minced

3 cups (540 g) green tomatoes, chopped

2 teaspoons fresh thyme

1 teaspoon dried rosemary

1 teaspoon sea salt

1 cup (200 g) French or green lentils, rinsed

juice of ½ lemon

4 cups (1 l) vegetable broth

⅓ cup (10 g), plus 1 tablespoon fresh parsley, finely chopped

1 In a stock pot or medium saucepan, heat the olive oil over medium heat and sauté the onion until translucent, about 5 minutes. Add the celery and garlic and cook for another minute or two, then add the tomatoes, thyme, rosemary, and salt. Continue to cook for another 5 to 7 minutes, until softened.

2 Add the lentils, lemon juice, and broth and bring to a boil. Reduce the heat to low, stir in ⅓ cup (10 g) parsley, and simmer uncovered for 20 to 30 minutes, until the lentils are tender. Add more liquid if necessary to stretch the broth. Garnish with the remaining fresh parsley and serve.

CALORIES (PER SERVING)	207
PROTEIN	12.6 g
TOTAL FAT	6.2 g
SATURATED FAT	1 g
CARBOHYDRATES	25.8 g
DIETARY FIBER	11.6 g
SUGARS	4.2 g
VITAMINS	B6, C

MEXICAN TORTILLA SOUP

 Serves 4–6 | gluten-free

Until a few years ago I had never had tortilla soup, as the restaurant versions aren't vegan. Now that I have had it, it's hard to imagine how I survived all those years without it! This meat-free version hits all the right marks: a little smoky, perfectly seasoned, and topped with creamy avocado and crunchy strips of corn tortillas.

Prep: 5 mins | Cook: 25 mins

1 dried ancho chili

1 tablespoon olive oil, plus 1 teaspoon for drizzling

1 small onion, diced

1 x 14 oz (400 g) can diced fire-roasted tomatoes

4½ cups (1.125 l) vegetable broth or vegan "chicken" broth

1 jalapeño pepper, seeded and minced

1 cup (170 g) cooked black beans (drained and rinsed, if canned)

4 corn tortillas

sea salt

1 avocado

1 lime

¼ cup (10 g) cilantro

2 cups (60 g) baby spinach

CALORIES (PER SERVING)	297
PROTEIN	13.3 g
TOTAL FAT	11.8 g
SATURATED FAT	2.4 g
CARBOHYDRATES	36.3 g
DIETARY FIBER	10 g
SUGARS	3.8 g
VITAMINS	B6

1 Pour 1 cup (250 ml) boiling water over the dried chili in a small dish and set aside.

2 In a stock pot or medium saucepan, heat 1 tablespoon of olive oil over medium heat, and add the onions, cooking until softened, about 5 minutes. Drain the chili and chop it into quarters. Add it to the onions, along with two-thirds of the canned tomatoes, and stir. Using an immersion blender, purée the contents of the pot until smooth. Alternatively, use a standing blender and then return to the pot.

3 Add the remaining tomatoes, broth, jalapeño, and black beans and bring to a boil. Reduce heat to low and simmer for 10 minutes.

4 Meanwhile, preheat the oven to 350°F (180°C). Stack the tortillas and cut them in half, then slice them into ½-inch (1-cm) wide strips. Place the strips on a baking sheet and drizzle with 1 teaspoon of oil. Bake for 8 to 10 minutes, then remove and sprinkle with a little sea salt while still warm.

5 Peel the avocado and cut the flesh into cubes. Squeeze the juice of ½ lime over it to keep it from browning. Cut the remaining lime into wedges. Wash and pat dry the cilantro.

6 When ready to serve, stir the spinach into the soup and allow it to wilt, then ladle the soup into shallow bowls. Top with crispy tortilla strips, avocado, and cilantro, with a wedge of lime on the side.

LEMONY MISO SOUP WITH CHINESE BROCCOLI

 Serves 4 / gluten-free

Fresh lemon juice brightens this miso soup, and Chinese broccoli adds both vibrancy of flavor and nutrition, packed as it is with vitamins A, C, K, folic acid, and dietary fiber. Add your favorite noodles to make a larger meal of it.

Prep: 10 mins | Cook: 10 mins

¼ cup (55 g) white miso paste
6 cups (1.5 l) water
2 tablespoons lemon juice
1½ cups (135 g) Chinese broccoli, chopped
½ cup (35 g) cremini mushrooms, sliced
½ cup (35 g) enoki mushrooms
1 green onion, sliced, to serve
thin slices of lemon, to serve

1 Whisk the miso paste with 1 cup (250 ml) hot water in a small bowl until the miso has dissolved. Add this mixture to a stock pot or medium saucepan along with the remaining water and lemon juice, and cook over medium heat to just below a boil. Add the broccoli and mushrooms and cook for 5 to 7 minutes, until the broccoli is tender.

2 To serve, ladle into bowls and top with green onion and a thin slice of fresh lemon.

GREEN TIP: If Chinese broccoli is unavailable, substitute regular broccoli or change the green all together and use 3 cups (100 g) chard.

CALORIES (PER SERVING)	45
PROTEIN	4.3 g
TOTAL FAT	1.3 g
SATURATED FAT	0.5 g
CARBOHYDRATES	8.5 g
DIETARY FIBER	0.8 g
SUGARS	3.4 g
VITAMINS	A, C, K

SWISS CHARD AND FARRO STEW

Serves 4-6

This is the kind of stick-to-your-ribs dish that I just want to dive into on a cold winter's day. If I had an Italian nona, I would like to think that she would approve of this soup. If using farro that has not been par-cooked, you will need to increase the cooking time to 40 minutes, or until it is tender.

Prep: 5 mins | Cook: 25 mins

1 tablespoon coconut oil

1 onion, diced

2 cloves garlic, minced

1 cup (160 g) farro (par-cooked)

3½ cups (875 ml) vegetable broth

1 x 14 oz (400 g) can diced tomatoes

½ bunch Swiss chard (about 4 cups (140 g) leaves and stems)

sea salt and freshly ground black pepper

(See image opposite, front)

1 Heat the coconut oil in a medium stock pot or saucepan over medium heat. Add the onion and garlic and sauté for 5 minutes, stirring regularly to keep the garlic from burning. Add the farro, stir to coat with oil, and continue to cook for 1 minute.

2 Add the broth and tomatoes. Bring the pot to a simmer, cover, and cook for 10 minutes.

3 While the soup is simmering, prepare the Swiss chard. Trim the stems from the leaves and dice the stems. Stack the leaves four at a time and roll them into a tight cigar. Slice thinly, so that you end up with long, thin ribbons of greens. Remove the lid from the pot and stir in the chard stalks. Cook until tender, about 4 to 5 minutes. Add the chard leaves, season to taste, stir, and cook for 2 more minutes. Serve hot with crusty bread.

CALORIES (PER SERVING)	167
PROTEIN	7.3 g
TOTAL FAT	3.6 g
SATURATED FAT	2.2 g
CARBOHYDRATES	26.5 g
DIETARY FIBER	3.6 g
SUGARS	3.7 g
VITAMINS	A, B6, C, K

RAW SUMMER SOUP

 Serves 3–4 / gluten-free

When it's too hot to cook, a chilled raw soup is just the thing you need. It's surprisingly filling with the avocado, and is full of vitamins, too. Enjoyed with a big fresh salad, it's the perfect meal for a midsummer's day.

Prep: 10 mins

2 avocados

1 sweet bell pepper (any color), seeds and membranes removed

1 cucumber

2 cups (60 g) baby greens (spinach, kale, arugula, etc.)

2–3 tablespoons fresh basil

juice of 1 lime

water

sprouts or micro-greens, to serve

(*See image, page 85, rear*)

1 Place the avocado, pepper, cucumber, greens, and basil in a food processor or blender along with the lime juice and ½ cup (120 ml) of water and process until smooth. Add more water, a tablespoon at a time, until a thick soup is achieved. Serve immediately, topped with fresh sprouts, or chill for up to 4 hours.

GREEN TIP: Try mixing up the tender greens and fresh herbs in this soup, depending on what's in your garden or what you find at the farmers' market. The combinations are endless (and delicious!)—try kale and dill, or spinach and chives.

CALORIES (PER SERVING)	143
PROTEIN	3.3 g
TOTAL FAT	10.7 g
SATURATED FAT	1.6 g
CARBOHYDRATES	12 g
DIETARY FIBER	6.4 g
SUGARS	3.3 g
VITAMINS	A, B6, C, K

WHITE BEAN AND THREE-GREEN SOUP

 Serves 2–4 / gluten-free

This velvety soup is rich in protein, thanks to the addition of beans, and features a powerhouse trifecta of greens: collard, spinach, and broccoli.

Prep: 10 mins | Cook: 15 mins

1 tablespoon olive oil

2 shallots, diced

1 x 14 oz (400 g) can white beans (white kidney or cannellini, etc.), drained and rinsed

3 cups (750 ml) vegetable broth or water

2 tablespoons nutritional yeast

1 teaspoon fresh rosemary

2 large collard green leaves, chopped

1 cup (30 g) spinach, chopped

1 cup (90 g) broccoli florets, chopped

sea salt and freshly ground black pepper

1 Heat the oil in a stock pot or saucepan over medium-high heat. Add the shallots and cook until soft, about 3 minutes. Add the beans, broth, nutritional yeast, and rosemary and bring to a boil. Reduce heat to low and simmer for 5 to 7 minutes.

2 Using either an immersion blender or a regular blender (in batches), purée until smooth. Return to the pan and return to a simmer. Add the greens and cook for 5 minutes, or until the broccoli is fork tender. Season to taste with sea salt and pepper, and serve, garnished with a sprig of rosemary if you'd like.

CALORIES (PER SERVING)	186
PROTEIN	13.3 g
TOTAL FAT	5 g
SATURATED FAT	0.9 g
CARBOHYDRATES	22.7 g
DIETARY FIBER	10.1 g
SUGARS	1.7 g
VITAMINS	A, C, K

CURRIED DAHL WITH CHARD

Serves 6 / gluten-free

Get ready for the earthy, warming spices of this soup, as zinc- and calcium-rich Swiss chard mixes and mingles with the ginger and lentils. Red lentils are so fast-cooking that this dish can be on the table in 20 minutes.

Prep: 5 mins | Cook: 20 mins

2 cups (400 g) red lentils, rinsed

2 tablespoons fresh ginger, minced

6 cups (1.5 l) water

½ bunch Swiss chard

3 tablespoons extra virgin olive oil

1 small onion, diced

3 teaspoons sea salt

2 teaspoons turmeric

1 teaspoon ground cumin

1 teaspoon ground coriander

1 large carrot, chopped

3 tablespoons tomato paste

1 x 14 oz (400 g) can coconut milk

2 green onions, diced

1 Place the lentils in a large stock pot or saucepan along with the ginger and water and bring to a boil over medium heat. Cover, reduce the heat to low, and simmer for 12 minutes, until the lentils are al dente.

2 Meanwhile, trim the stems from the chard leaves and dice the stems. Stack the leaves four at a time and roll them into a tight cigar. Slice thinly, so that you end up with long ribbons of greens.

3 Heat the oil in a small frying pan and sauté the onion until starting to brown. Add the salt and spices and cook for 1 minute, stirring. Scrape this into the pot along with the diced chard stems, carrots, tomato paste, coconut milk, and stir well. Bring the soup back to a simmer for another 5 minutes, then fold in the Swiss chard leaves and cook for 3 to 4 minutes until the lentils are soft and broken down. Ladle into bowls and serve topped with green onions.

GREEN TIP: This soup will thicken into a lovely stew as it sits. Enjoy the leftovers this way over your favorite grain, or simply thin it out with more water or a little vegetable broth.

CALORIES (PER SERVING)	458
PROTEIN	19.8 g
TOTAL FAT	22.2 g
SATURATED FAT	13.7 g
CARBOHYDRATES	48.8 g
DIETARY FIBER	22.2 g
SUGARS	3.9 g
VITAMINS	A, B6, C, K

MY FAVORITE FOUR-INGREDIENT SALAD

 Serves 2–3 / gluten-free

That's a bold statement for sure, but this salad lives up to its name. With only four ingredients, it's simplicity at its best. It can hold its own for flavor, but the best part about this salad is that it can be the base for much more—add grilled tofu, crunchy baked chickpeas, farm-fresh vegetables, seeds, and nuts, whatever your heart desires! I believe it will soon become your favorite salad, too.

Prep: 10 mins

6 cups (420 g) kale
1 avocado
1 tablespoon umeboshi vinegar
2 tablespoons nutritional yeast

1 Wash and dry the kale. Remove the tough ribs with a sharp knife, then stack the leaves and slice them into ribbons. Place them in a large salad bowl and add the flesh of the avocado. Mash the avocado with a fork and then, using your hands, massage it into the greens, really working it all in. Do this for a few minutes until the kale has tenderized and reduced in volume.

2 Drizzle the vinegar over the top of the salad and sprinkle with the nutritional yeast. Toss the salad and serve.

GREEN TIP: Don't skip the step where you massage the kale. By doing this, you work the oil right into the leaves, breaking down some of the kale's tough texture, making it much more pleasing to eat raw.

CALORIES (PER SERVING)	226
PROTEIN	8.3 g
TOTAL FAT	13.4 g
SATURATED FAT	2.8 g
CARBOHYDRATES	22.8 g
DIETARY FIBER	8.2 g
SUGARS	0 g
VITAMINS	A, B6, C, K

SPINACH GOMAE

Serves 4 / gluten-free

When I lived in Vancouver I would stop by the same little sushi joint at least twice a week for an avocado roll and spinach gomae salad. I became seriously obsessed with the salad and took it upon myself to recreate it. I use tahini instead of grinding my own sesame paste, which makes it that much quicker to prepare.

Prep: 5 mins | Cook: 5 mins

1 lb (450 g) fresh spinach, washed

⅓ cup (85 g) tahini

¼ cup (60 ml) gluten-free tamari

1 tablespoon sesame oil

water

2 tablespoons toasted sesame seeds

(*See image below, front*)

1 Bring a large pan of water to a boil and submerge the spinach briefly, cooking it for only 10 to 20 seconds. Drain, then plunge the spinach into a bowl of iced water to stop the cooking process. Drain again.

2 Gather the spinach by the stems and gently wring out any excess water. Chop into thirds (or quarters if the stems are quite long) and place in a bowl.

3 Combine the tahini, tamari, sesame oil, and enough water to make a thick dressing; about 2 to 3 tablespoons should be about adequate.

4 Toss the spinach with three-quarters of the dressing, aiming to coat all the leaves.

5 Divide between four plates and drizzle with the remaining dressing. Sprinkle with sesame seeds and serve.

CALORIES (PER SERVING)	212
PROTEIN	9.3 g
TOTAL FAT	16.9 g
SATURATED FAT	2.4 g
CARBOHYDRATES	10.4 g
DIETARY FIBER	5 g
SUGARS	0.9 g
VITAMINS	A, C, K

BEET GREENS, PEAR, AND MAPLE WALNUT SALAD

 Serves 2-3 | gluten-free

The sweet pear and candied walnuts are a great contrast to the beet greens in this salad. In addition to the maple walnuts adding a sweet, crunchy topping, they are also full of heart-healthy omega-3s.

Prep: 5 mins | Cook: 60 mins

1 bunch beets with greens (about 3–5 beets)
2–3 cups (90 g) mixed salad greens
2 tablespoons maple syrup
½ cup (50 g) walnuts
2 tablespoons olive oil
1 tablespoon balsamic vinegar
1 teaspoon Dijon mustard
1 teaspoon lemon juice
1 pear, cored and sliced
sea salt and freshly ground black pepper
(*See image, opposite, rear*)

1 Preheat the oven to 400°F (200°C). Remove the beet greens about an inch (2.5 cm) from the beetroot. Wash the beets, then wrap them each in tinfoil (if beets are really small they can all be packaged together) and place in the oven for 50 to 60 minutes, or until easily pierced by a fork. Once cool enough to handle, rub the skins off with a paper towel (to save your hands from staining) and dice.

2 While the beets are roasting, prepare the rest of the salad. Trim and discard the tough stems from the beet greens and wash and dry the leaves. Chop them into 2-inch (5-cm) pieces.

3 Candy the walnuts by heating the maple syrup in a small frying pan over medium-high heat until it begins to bubble. Add the walnuts and stir to coat in the syrup. Continue cooking and stirring for 4 to 5 minutes, until the syrup has caramelized the walnuts and cooked off. Remove from the heat. The walnuts will be sticky, but do your best to separate them with the spatula, sprinkle with a pinch of sea salt, and leave in the pan to cool and harden.

4 Combine the olive oil, balsamic vinegar, mustard, and lemon juice, and season to taste.

5 To assemble the salad, place the beet green leaves, walnuts, and pear in a bowl. Add the dressing, and toss well. The diced beets will turn everything pink (unless you are using golden or candy cane beets), so to avoid this, leave the beets out while tossing and add at the end.

CALORIES (PER SERVING)	316
PROTEIN	7.3 g
TOTAL FAT	19.4 g
SATURATED FAT	1.9 g
CARBOHYDRATES	33.1 g
DIETARY FIBER	5.3 g
SUGARS	19.4 g
VITAMINS	C

GREEN BEAN AND MANGO SALAD

Serves 6 | gluten-free

Whenever I go out for Thai food, I always order a mango salad, but I do wish it contained more greens, other than a sprig or two of cilantro. This salad fixes that with lots of folate-rich green beans.

Prep: 10 mins | Cook: 5 mins

3 cups (450 g) green beans

2 slightly underripe mangos

1 cup (150 g) cherry or grape tomatoes, halved

¼ cup (10 g) fresh cilantro

3 green onions, sliced

¼ cup (35 g) peanuts, crushed

1 tablespoon vegetable oil

2 tablespoons fresh lime juice

1 tablespoon gluten-free tamari

½ teaspoon unrefined cane sugar

1 fresh Thai chili, minced (optional)

(See image below, left)

1 Bring a pan of water to a boil. Add the green beans and cook for up to 2 minutes, until bright green and tender crisp. Drain, then plunge them into a bowl of iced water to halt the cooking process. Drain again. Trim the ends and slice them in half lengthwise. Place them in a large bowl and set aside.

2 Peel the mango and slice into long, thin strips. Add this to the green beans, along with the tomatoes, cilantro, onion, and peanuts.

3 Whisk together the remaining ingredients to make a dressing. Pour over the salad, toss, and serve. The salad can be made and dressed ahead of time and left to chill and marinate in the fridge for up to 3 hours.

GREEN TIP: If Asian long beans are available, try using them in place of the green beans.

CALORIES (PER SERVING)	117
PROTEIN	4 g
TOTAL FAT	5.7 g
SATURATED FAT	1 g
CARBOHYDRATES	15.3 g
DIETARY FIBER	4.4 g
SUGARS	7.8 g
VITAMINS	C

RUSTIC PANZANELLA WITH BRUSSELS SPROUTS AND ARTICHOKES

 Serves 4–6 | gluten-free option

Traditional panzanella is made with stale bread, onions, and tomatoes, but we're giving it a green makeover and using Brussels sprouts, sugar snap peas, and artichoke hearts. It's a thing of beauty. If you'd like, you can use gluten-free bread as an alternative.

Prep: 10 mins | Cook: 35 mins

2 cups (180 g) Brussels sprouts
5 tablespoons olive oil
½ loaf day-old multigrain bread
1 clove garlic, minced
1 teaspoon fresh thyme
1 cup (100 g) sugar snap peas
1 cup (170 g) artichoke hearts, quartered
⅓ cup (15 g) fresh basil leaves, torn
2 tablespoons sherry vinegar
2 teaspoons Dijon mustard
sea salt and freshly ground black pepper
(See image, opposite, right)

1 Preheat the oven to 400°F (200°C). Cut the Brussels sprouts in half, remove any browned outside leaves, and toss with 1 tablespoon of the olive oil in a bowl. Spread out on a baking sheet and sprinkle with a pinch of sea salt and a few cracks of fresh pepper. Place in the oven and roast for 30 to 35 minutes, until golden brown.

2 Cut the bread into large, 2-inch (5-cm) cubes. Heat another tablespoon of oil in a skillet and add the garlic, cooking until fragrant, about 1 minute. Add the bread, the fresh thyme, and a pinch of salt. Cook over medium-high heat for 8 to 10 minutes, stirring occasionally to toast all sides. Remove from heat.

3 Trim the peas and add them to a large bowl along with the artichoke hearts, Brussels sprouts, bread, and basil.

4 In a bowl, combine the sherry vinegar, mustard, and remaining olive oil. Just before serving, toss the sherry vinaigrette through the salad.

CALORIES (PER SERVING)	243
PROTEIN	8 g
TOTAL FAT	13.7 g
SATURATED FAT	2.1 g
CARBOHYDRATES	24.9 g
DIETARY FIBER	6.1 g
SUGARS	4 g
VITAMINS	C

CAESAR SALAD WITH TEMPEH "BACON"

Serves 4 / gluten-free

Is there anything better than a crisp Caesar salad? Try this one on for size. It has a nice balance of romaine lettuce and kale, with lots of tempeh "bacon." The creamy dressing is made with silken tofu, so it's high in protein, too.

Prep: 10 mins | Cook: 20 mins

1 romaine heart
4–5 kale leaves, stems removed
1 batch Tempeh "Bacon"
(page 43)

FOR THE CREAMY CAESAR DRESSING
¼ cup (60 g) silken tofu
1 tablespoon olive oil
2 tablespoons nutritional yeast
1 tablespoon capers
1 tablespoon caper brine
2 teaspoons Dijon mustard
1½ teaspoons white miso
½ teaspoon kelp granules
¼ teaspoon garlic powder
¼ teaspoon sea salt
freshly ground black pepper
(*See image, rear*)

1 Wash and dry the romaine and kale leaves. Tear the romaine into large pieces. Stack the kale leaves, roll them tightly, and slice them into thin ribbons. Set aside.

2 For the dressing, mix all the ingredients together using a blender or food processor.

3 Place the kale and 2 tablespoons of the dressing in a salad bowl. Massage the dressing into the kale for 1 to 2 minutes. Add the romaine lettuce and more dressing. Toss well, divide between four plates, and top with crumbled tempeh bacon.

CALORIES (PER SERVING)	152
PROTEIN	10.8 g
TOTAL FAT	7.6 g
SATURATED FAT	1.3 g
CARBOHYDRATES	13.5 g
DIETARY FIBER	2.3 g
SUGARS	3.4 g
VITAMINS	A, C

KALE WALDORF SALAD WITH AVOCADO ASTORIA DRESSING

 Serves 6 / gluten-free

Named after the grand Waldorf Astoria Hotel in New York, but with a bit of a revamp. Given that many consider kale to be the Queen of Greens, I suppose a luxurious salad such as this is fitting.

Prep: 10 mins

1 bunch kale (curly or lacinato)
1 apple, cored and cubed
½ cup (45 g) red seedless grapes, halved
3 ribs celery, chopped
⅔ cup (65 g) walnut halves

FOR THE AVOCADO ASTORIA DRESSING

1 avocado
2 teaspoons Dijon mustard
1 tablespoon apple cider vinegar
½ teaspoon dried dill
water
sea salt
(*See image, opposite, front*)

1 Wash and dry the kale. Remove the tough ribs with a sharp knife, then stack the leaves and slice them into ribbons.

2 Combine the kale, apple, grapes, celery, and walnuts in a large salad bowl.

3 For the dressing, scoop the flesh of the avocado into a bowl and mash it well with a fork. Whisk in the mustard, vinegar, and dill. The dressing will be very thick, so thin it out with a little water, adding 1 tablespoon at a time; about 3 to 4 tablespoons should do the trick. Season to taste with sea salt.

4 Add the dressing to the salad bowl and toss well to coat. Serve immediately, or cover and refrigerate for up to 3 hours until ready to serve.

CALORIES (PER SERVING)	198
PROTEIN	5.4 g
TOTAL FAT	14.8 g
SATURATED FAT	1.9 g
CARBOHYDRATES	15 g
DIETARY FIBER	5 g
SUGARS	6 g
VITAMINS	A, B6, C

SHREDDED RAINBOW SALAD WITH LEMONY AVOCADO DRESSING

 Serves 4–6 / gluten-free

Eating greens can be colorful, too! This bright, crunchy salad will excite your eyes as much as your taste buds, and is perfect for a potluck or a big backyard family meal. Because of the heartiness of the vegetables in this salad, which don't wilt when dressed, it can be made in advance and refrigerated, or kept as leftovers for the next day.

Prep: 10 mins | Cook: 5 mins

½ small red cabbage

2 carrots

3–4 kale leaves, stems removed

½ cucumber

1 cup (150 g) shelled frozen edamame

3 tablespoons shelled hemp seeds

FOR THE LEMONY AVOCADO DRESSING

1 small avocado

2 tablespoons fresh cilantro

¼ cup (60 ml) water

2 tablespoons lemon juice

¼ teaspoon sea salt

1 Shred or grate all the vegetables either by hand or using a food processor fitted with the grating blade.

2 Bring a small pot of water to a boil. Cook the edamame in boiling water for 3 to 4 minutes. Strain and rinse in cool water to stop the cooking process.

3 Combine all the shredded vegetables in a large bowl along with the edamame and 2 tablespoons hemp hearts.

4 For the dressing, combine all ingredients in a food processor and blend until silky smooth.

5 Add the lemony avocado dressing to the vegetables and toss well. Store any leftover dressing in a covered container in the fridge for up to three days.

6 Garnish with the last tablespoon of hemp seeds. Serve at room temperature.

CALORIES (PER SERVING)	174
PROTEIN	7.2 g
TOTAL FAT	10.1 g
SATURATED FAT	1.7 g
CARBOHYDRATES	16.1 g
DIETARY FIBER	6.4 g
SUGARS	3.4 g
VITAMINS	A, B6, C

MEDITERRANEAN BROCCOLI AND BARLEY SALAD

 Serves 3-4

Cold grain salads are right up my alley, and I just love the chewiness that barley offers—it's a really nice contrast to the bright, crisp broccoli. This dish is high in fiber and protein and has loads of vitamins A, C, and K.

Prep: 10 mins | Cook: 40 mins

1 cup (250 g) pot barley, rinsed

3 cups (750 ml) water

2 cups (180 g) broccoli, chopped

3–4 kale leaves, stems removed

¼ cup (15 g) sundried tomatoes in oil, drained and sliced

½ cup (50 g) black olives, pitted and chopped

2 tablespoons olive oil

1½ tablespoons lemon juice

sea salt and freshly ground black pepper

1 Put the pot barley in a pan with the water and bring to a rolling boil. Reduce the heat to low, cover, and let simmer for 40 minutes, or until tender and all the water has been absorbed. Remove from the heat, fluff with a fork, and allow to cool.

2 While the barley is cooking, bring a pan of salted water to a boil. Add the broccoli and cook for 1 minute over medium heat. Drain, then plunge directly into a bowl of iced water. Let the broccoli sit for 1 minute, then drain and pat dry. Stack the kale leaves and slice them into ribbons.

3 Transfer the barley to a serving bowl along with the broccoli, kale, sundried tomatoes, and olives. Whisk together the oil and lemon juice, season to taste with salt and pepper, then pour over the bowl. Toss well and serve.

GREEN TIP: When a salad is made with hearty greens such as broccoli and kale, it can be made well ahead of time as they will not wilt easily even when dressed.

CALORIES (PER SERVING)	333
PROTEIN	8.9 g
TOTAL FAT	9.4 g
SATURATED FAT	1.4 g
CARBOHYDRATES	57.1 g
DIETARY FIBER	12.2 g
SUGARS	2.8 g
VITAMINS	A, C, K

ARUGULA, WATERCRESS, AND STONE-FRUIT SALAD WITH JALAPEÑO VINAIGRETTE

 Serves 4–6 / gluten-free

Sweet, ripe fruits like peaches, plums, and nectarines are the perfect complement to peppery herbs like arugula and watercress. The dressing is very mild, so if you are looking to add a bit more heat, feel free to leave in some or all of the jalapeño pepper seeds.

Prep: 15 mins

3 cups (60 g) arugula

3 cups (100 g) watercress

½ cucumber, sliced

1 peach or nectarine, pitted and sliced

1 plum, pitted and sliced (optional)

½ cup (50 g) pecans, toasted

¼ cup (40 g) red onion, thinly sliced

FOR THE JALAPEÑO VINAIGRETTE

1 jalapeño, seeds and membranes removed, chopped

2 tablespoons olive oil

2 tablespoons orange juice

1 tablespoon white wine vinegar

pinch of sea salt

1 Combine all the salad ingredients in a serving bowl.

2 Blend the vinaigrette ingredients until smooth. Pour over the salad, toss, and serve. Alternatively, this salad lends itself beautifully to individually plated portions. Simply plate each salad, then drizzle each portion with the vinaigrette.

CALORIES (PER SERVING)	126
PROTEIN	2.1 g
TOTAL FAT	10.9 g
SATURATED FAT	1.3 g
CARBOHYDRATES	6.7 g
DIETARY FIBER	2 g
SUGARS	3.8 g
VITAMINS	B6, C

SUPERFOOD SALAD

Serves 2-3 / gluten-free

Some of my favorite superfoods make up this salad—from nutrient-dense kale to pumpkin and hemp seeds to goji berries, it's like a little superfood party in the salad bowl. Baby kale and chard are sometimes available at the supermarket in pre-packaged form. Their leaves tend to be a little more tender and they are often triple-washed, which can save time in the prep department.

Prep: 15 mins

6 cups (180 g) blend of baby kale and baby chard

1 cup (230 g) cooked adzuki beans (drained and rinsed, if canned)

1 cup (85 g) pea shoots

1 cup (85 g) sunflower sprouts

½ cup (75 g) grape tomatoes, halved

⅓ cup (30 g) walnuts

¼ cup (35 g) pumpkin seeds

2 tablespoons goji berries

2 tablespoons shelled hemp seeds

1 batch of your favorite dressing (my personal favorite for this salad is the Lemony Avocado Dressing on page 98)

(See image, rear)

1 Combine all the salad ingredients in a serving bowl. Toss with your favorite dressing and serve.

GREEN TIP: Mature greens will also work in this salad, however, you will need to slice them thinly and massage them with a few drops of olive oil prior to assembling the salad.

CALORIES (PER SERVING)	
(SALAD ONLY)	337
PROTEIN	17.1 g
TOTAL FAT	16.0 g
SATURATED FAT	1.7 g
CARBOHYDRATES	36 g
DIETARY FIBER	9.7 g
SUGARS	4.5 g
VITAMINS	A, C, K

SHAVED BRUSSELS SPROUT SALAD WITH HEMP AND ORANGE

 Serves 4 / gluten-free

I have a serious love of Brussels sprouts. Usually I roast them, but after trying them shredded in this salad I discovered how amazing they are raw, too. Like all brassica-family veggies they are chock full of antioxidants and blood-healthy vitamin K, and the avocado and hemp offer heart-healthy omega fats.

Prep: 10 mins

3 cups (270 g) Brussels sprouts

2 cups (40 g) arugula

1 orange

1 avocado

¼ cup (35 g) shelled hemp seeds

3 tablespoons olive oil

2 tablespoons lemon juice

1 teaspoon agave or maple syrup

sea salt and freshly ground black pepper

(*See image, opposite, front*)

1 Peel any browned leaves from the sprouts, but don't trim their ends—this gives you something to hold onto. Shave the sprouts finely, then place them in a large salad bowl with the arugula. Peel and dice the orange and avocado and add them to the bowl with the hemp seeds.

2 Mix the remaining ingredients together to create a simple vinaigrette, season to taste, then toss into the salad and serve.

GREEN TIP: There's more than one way to shave a Brussels sprout. Use a mandolin and box grater, a food processor fitted with the slicing attachment, or by hand with a sharp knife.

CALORIES (PER SERVING)	271
PROTEIN	7.7 g
TOTAL FAT	21.7 g
SATURATED FAT	3.2 g
CARBOHYDRATES	17.6 g
DIETARY FIBER	8.2 g
SUGARS	7.5 g
VITAMINS	C

GREEN ENTRÉES

ZUCCHINI NOODLE BOLOGNESE

 Serves 4 / gluten-free

Try this take on the classic Italian dish that sees zucchini moonlighting as pasta, and mushrooms filling in for the classic meat sauce. If you have a vegetable spiralizer or julienne tool you can make use of it here; if not, just use a vegetable peeler to create long, thin "noodles."

Prep: 10 mins | Cook: 35 mins

5–6 small zucchini
2 tablespoons olive oil
1 onion, chopped
2 large carrots, chopped
4 ribs celery, chopped
8 cremini mushrooms, chopped
¼ cup (60 ml) dry white wine
1 x 28 oz (800 g) can whole or diced tomatoes
½ teaspoon dried oregano
½ teaspoon dried basil
sea salt and freshly ground black pepper

1 Slice, julienne, or spiralize the zucchini into noodles. Aim for 2 to 3 cups of noodles per serving. Set aside.

2 In a large skillet, heat the oil, then add the onion and sauté until translucent, about 5 minutes. Add the carrots, celery, and mushrooms and continue to cook over medium-high heat for 10 minutes, stirring regularly. The vegetables will cook down and soften. Add the wine and stir for 3 to 4 minutes as it cooks off.

3 Purée the tomatoes and add them to the pan along with the oregano and basil. Simmer, uncovered, for 12 to 15 minutes, until the sauce has thickened, then remove from the heat and season to taste.

4 Meanwhile, bring a pot of salted water to a boil. Add the zucchini noodles and cook for 30 to 60 seconds. Then drain, divide the noodles between four plates and top each with a ladle of the veggie Bolognese sauce.

GREEN TIP: Zucchini noodles are just as enjoyable uncooked. For a delicious raw alternative, try tossing them with fresh pesto.

CALORIES (PER SERVING)	196
PROTEIN	6.8 g
TOTAL FAT	7.6 g
SATURATED FAT	1.1 g
CARBOHYDRATES	27 g
DIETARY FIBER	7.3 g
SUGARS	13.7 g
VITAMINS	A, B6, C

KELP NOODLE AND TAHINI TANGLE WITH MISO TAHINI DRESSING

 Serves 2 / gluten-free

A big ol' bowl of crunchy, raw goodness. There's plenty of protein kicking around too, from the hemp seeds, cashews, and tahini. If kelp noodles are unavailable, substitute with rice vermicelli or udon noodles (udon noodles are *not* gluten-free).

Prep: 10 mins

1 x 12 oz (340 g) bag kelp noodles
3 cups (225 g) lactino kale
⅓ cucumber, seeded and diced
2 ribs celery, sliced
1 carrot, grated
2 tablespoons shelled hemp seeds
¼ cup (40 g) toasted cashews

FOR THE MISO TAHINI DRESSING

2 teaspoons white miso paste
2 tablespoons tahini
1 tablespoon gluten-free tamari
1 teaspoon sesame oil
1 teaspoon umeboshi vinegar
dash of agave nectar
2 tablespoons water
(*See image, opposite, front*)

1 Rinse the kelp noodles in a colander. Using your hands, separate the noodles, snipping them with kitchen scissors to shorten them to a more manageable length, as they do become quite tangled when left long.

2 Wash and dry the kale. Remove the tough ribs with a sharp knife, then stack the leaves and slice them into ribbons. Place the kale and the noodles in a large serving bowl and set aside.

3 For the dressing, whisk all the ingredients together. As with all sauces calling for nut or seed butter, the dressing will thicken up before it thins to the consistency you're after. After mixing, if the dressing is still too thick for your liking, add water a teaspoon at a time until the desired consistency is reached.

4 Add half the dressing to the noodles, tossing well to coat.

5 Add the cucumber, celery, carrot, hemp seeds, and cashews to the bowl. Top with the remaining dressing, mix, and serve.

CALORIES (PER SERVING)	364
PROTEIN	13 g
TOTAL FAT	20.1 g
SATURATED FAT	3.3 g
CARBOHYDRATES	38.6 g
DIETARY FIBER	7.4 g
SUGARS	6.4 g
VITAMINS	A, C

SPICY PEANUT NOODLE BOWL

Serves 4 / gluten-free option

It is my opinion that everyone should know how to make a good peanut sauce. This dish is my go-to for cleaning out the vegetable drawer before my next organic produce delivery arrives. For a gluten-free option, use gluten-free soba noodles.

Prep: 5 mins | Cook: 20 mins

1 x 1 lb (454 g) pack soba noodles

4 cups (360 g) broccoli, chopped

1½ cups (150 g) snow peas, trimmed

2 green onions, diced

FOR THE PEANUT SAUCE

3 teaspoons toasted sesame oil

2½ tablespoons rice vinegar

¼ cup (60 ml) gluten-free tamari

⅓ cup (80 g) natural peanut butter

½ cup (125 ml) water

2 tablespoons Sriracha or other chili sauce

(See image, rear)

1 Cook the soba noodles according to the package directions. When there is 1 minute of cooking time left, add the broccoli. Drain the noodles and broccoli and rinse with cold water to stop the cooking process and remove the excess starch from the soba.

2 For the peanut sauce, combine the sesame oil, rice vinegar, and tamari in a small pan and warm over medium-low heat for 1 minute. Add the peanut butter and stir gently for 2 to 3 minutes as it softens and melts. Add the water slowly until the sauce has reached a smooth consistency. Continue to stir for 3 to 4 minutes as it simmers and thickens. Add some or all of the Sriracha to create as much or as little heat as you like.

3 Remove the spicy peanut sauce from the heat and toss in a large serving bowl with the soba noodles, broccoli, snow peas, and green onions.

CALORIES (PER SERVING)	613
PROTEIN	27.7 g
TOTAL FAT	15.4 g
SATURATED FAT	2.9 g
CARBOHYDRATES	100.7 g
DIETARY FIBER	5.1 g
SUGARS	6 g
VITAMINS	B6, C

GINGER BOK CHOY AND SWEET PEAS WITH MISO-GLAZED TOFU

 Serves 3–4 | gluten-free

I really do love the combination of fresh ginger and toasted sesame oil, especially with bok choy. This dish is rich in vitamins A and K, as well as calcium and dietary fiber.

Prep: 10 mins | Cook: 20 mins

1 x 16 oz (454 g) pack extra-firm tofu

2 tablespoons white miso paste

2 tablespoons mirin

1 tablespoon water

2 teaspoons vegetable oil

4–5 heads baby bok choy

2 tablespoons toasted sesame oil

1-inch (2.5-cm) piece fresh ginger, minced

2 cups (200 g) sugar snap peas

cooked quinoa, to serve

1 Slice the tofu across the width into 12 thin pieces. Pat dry with a paper towel. Whisk together the miso, half the mirin, water, and vegetable oil. Coat the tofu slices in the miso mixture and spread them out on a baking sheet lined with aluminum foil. Broil on the middle rack of the oven for 6 to 8 minutes on each side, until golden and crispy at the edges, watching closely to ensure it doesn't burn.

2 Slice each bok choy in half. Trim the root ends and remove the tough core with a paring knife. Heat the sesame oil in a large frying pan and add the ginger, cooking for 1 minute, until fragrant. Add the bok choy, cut-side down, to sear for 3 minutes. Flip over and sear the topside for another 2 minutes.

3 Increase the heat to high, add the peas and remaining tablespoon of mirin, and cover for 1 minute to finish cooking. Serve with the miso-glazed tofu and quinoa.

CALORIES (PER SERVING)	348
PROTEIN	28 g
TOTAL FAT	16.7 g
SATURATED FAT	2.7 g
CARBOHYDRATES	35.7 g
DIETARY FIBER	12.9 g
SUGARS	18.7 g
VITAMINS	A, B6, C

ORECCHIETTE WITH CHARD, SUNDRIED TOMATOES, AND TOASTED ALMONDS

Serves 4 / gluten-free option

This pasta is a crowd-pleaser, perfect for family dinners. The slightly bitter chard combined with the salty sundried tomatoes is a perfect match. For a gluten-free option, use your favorite gluten-free pasta.

Prep: 10 mins | Cook: 25 mins

¼ cup (40 g) almonds

1 bunch Swiss chard

4 tablespoons olive oil

2 tablespoons chopped garlic

1 x 28 oz (800 g) can diced tomatoes, puréed

½ cup (30 g) sundried tomatoes (not in oil), sliced

1 x 1 lb (454 g) pack orecchiette pasta

sea salt and freshly ground black pepper

toasted almonds, to serve

1 Cover a baking sheet in parchment paper, and spread the almonds over the sheet. Place under the broiler for 5 minutes, watching them very closely and stirring every minute or so. Once they begin to brown on all sides, remove them from the broiler. Once cool, chop them into small pieces and set aside.

2 Meanwhile, trim the stems from the chard leaves and dice the stems. Stack the leaves four at a time and roll them into a tight cigar. Slice thinly, so that you end up with long, thin ribbons of greens.

3 In a large skillet, heat 2 tablespoons of the oil and add the garlic, stirring frequently so that it doesn't brown. After 1 to 2 minutes, add the chard stems and sauté for 5 minutes until softened, then add the chard greens and a generous pinch of sea salt and continue to cook the chard for 3 to 4 minutes, until wilted. Transfer to a bowl.

4 Return the skillet to the heat and add the remaining oil, puréed tomatoes, and sundried tomatoes, and simmer for 15 minutes. The sundried tomatoes will rehydrate in the sauce, adding to the depth of flavor. Return the chard to the pan, season to taste, and heat through.

5 Cook the pasta according to package directions and then add it to the sauce. Serve hot, topped with toasted almonds.

CALORIES (PER SERVING)	694
PROTEIN	21.2 g
TOTAL FAT	21.6 g
SATURATED FAT	2.4 g
CARBOHYDRATES	107.9 g
DIETARY FIBER	8.9 g
SUGARS	12.4 g
VITAMINS	A, C, K

LINGUINI WITH LEMON, OLIVES, AND RAPINI

 Serves 4 / gluten-free option

There's nothing too fancy here, just simple, good flavors—garlic, lemon, rapini, and briney olives. For a gluten-free option, use your favorite gluten-free pasta.

Prep: 5 mins | Cook: 15 mins

1 bunch rapini

2 tablespoons olive oil, plus extra to serve

1 tablespoon minced garlic

¼ cup (60 ml) lemon juice

¼ cup (60 ml) dry white wine

¼ cup (45 g) capers, drained

½ cup (50 g) good-quality olives

sea salt and freshly ground black pepper

1 x 1 lb (454 g) pack linguini

1 Chop the rapini, separating the stems from the tender greens. Bring a medium pot of water to a boil and add the stems for 1 minute, then add the greens for a further minute. Drain and set aside.

2 Heat the oil in a large sauté pan and add the garlic. Cook for 1 to 2 minutes, stirring frequently so that it doesn't brown, then add the rapini, lemon juice, and wine and raise the heat to high. Simmer for 3 to 4 minutes until reduced by half, then add the capers and olives, stir, and remove from the heat.

3 Meanwhile, cook the pasta according to package directions. Drain, reserving ¼ cup (50 ml) of the cooking water. Add the pasta to the sauce along with the reserved cooking water. Toss the pasta in the pan to coat with the sauce, drizzle with more olive oil, if you like, then season lightly with salt and freshly ground black pepper, and serve.

GREEN TIP: Rapini is also known as broccoli rabe, so if you can't find it under one name while shopping, look for the other!

CALORIES (PER SERVING)	535
PROTEIN	16.2 g
TOTAL FAT	11.3 g
SATURATED FAT	1.1 g
CARBOHYDRATES	85.8 g
DIETARY FIBER	2.4 g
SUGARS	5.1 g
VITAMINS	A, C

CHARD, CILANTRO, AND CASHEW "CHEESE" PIZZA

 Serves 2-3

Pesto-covered pizzas are a really nice change from the usual tomato-based versions, and broccoli on pizza is always a good idea in my book. This recipe is kid-approved too.

Prep: 10 mins | Cook: 12 to 15 mins

cornmeal for sprinkling

1 x 14 oz (400 g) pack prepared pizza dough

1 cup (250 ml) Chard and Cilantro Pesto (page 74)

1 cup (90 g) broccoli florets, chopped

¼ cup (40 g) red onion, sliced

½ cup Cashew "Cheese" (page 66)

(*See image, front*)

1 Preheat the oven to 450°F (230°C). Grease a large baking sheet. On a surface sprinkled with cornmeal, roll out the dough to a 12-inch (30-cm) circle, then place it on the baking sheet.

2 Spread pesto over the stretched dough, leaving a border around the edge. Top with the broccoli, red onions, and teaspoon-sized dollops of cashew "cheese." Bake for 12 to 15 minutes, or until the crust is lightly browned. Slice and serve.

GREEN TIP: The Kale and Walnut Pesto (page 74) can also be used in this recipe, and yields equally delicious results.

CALORIES (PER SERVING)	662
PROTEIN	21.5 g
TOTAL FAT	27.7 g
SATURATED FAT	5 g
CARBOHYDRATES	88.9 g
DIETARY FIBER	8.9 g
SUGARS	3.1 g
VITAMINS	B6

SUNDRIED TOMATO AND ARUGULA PIZZA

 Serves 2-3

Around the time I got married, I was working at a little Italian restaurant in our neighborhood. At least once a week during a dinner shift, my husband would show up to order a pizza and it was always the same thing: one of their Prosciutto-Arugula pizzas but with sundried tomatoes instead of the meat. It quickly became known as the "Mark special" and continues to be one of our favorite flavor combinations for pizza night.

Prep: 10 mins | Cook: 12 to 15 mins

cornmeal for sprinkling

1 x 14 oz (400 g) prepared pizza dough

½ cup (30 g) sundried tomatoes in oil

3 cups (60 g) arugula

FOR THE QUICK PIZZA SAUCE

1 cup (250 ml) Italian tomato passata (or 1 cup (250 ml) puréed canned tomatoes, plus 1 tablespoon tomato paste)

1 teaspoon olive oil

½ teaspoon dried oregano

¼ teaspoon sea salt

1 tablespoon chopped fresh basil

(*See image, opposite, rear*)

1 Preheat the oven to 450°F (230°C). Grease a large baking sheet. On a surface sprinkled with cornmeal, roll out the dough to a 12-inch (30-cm) circle, then place it on the baking sheet.

2 For the pizza sauce, combine all the ingredients together. Spread the sauce over the stretched dough, leaving a border around the edge. Top with the sundried tomatoes. Bake for 12 to 15 minutes, or until the crust is lightly browned. Remove from oven and immediately top with arugula. Let sit for 5 minutes, then slice and serve.

CALORIES (PER SERVING)	404
PROTEIN	14.7 g
TOTAL FAT	5.6 g
SATURATED FAT	1.4 g
CARBOHYDRATES	76.3 g
DIETARY FIBER	7.4 g
SUGARS	2.4 g
VITAMINS	K

SHAVED ASPARAGUS AND ROASTED TOMATO TARTINE

 Serves 2

Tartine is just a fancy word for an open sandwich, but eating ribbons of raw asparagus makes me feel oh-so-fancy, so I'm embracing tartine.

Prep: 5 mins | Cook: 15 mins

1½ cups (225 g) cherry or grape tomatoes on the vine

1 tablespoon olive oil

2 small, ripe avocados

wedge of lemon

6 asparagus spears

4 slices good, crusty sourdough bread

sea salt

1 Preheat the oven to 400°F (200°C). Separate the tomatoes into clusters of three or four by snipping the vines carefully with kitchen scissors. Place them in a roasting pan, drizzle with olive oil, and sprinkle with a generous pinch of sea salt. Roast in the oven for 10 to 15 minutes, or until they collapse. Remove and cool to room temperature.

2 Scoop the flesh from the avocados into a bowl and mash gently with a fork. Squeeze the wedge of lemon over the top and mash again to keep it from browning.

3 Snap the woody ends off the asparagus spears, then, using a vegetable peeler, carefully shave the asparagus into ribbons.

4 To assemble, toast the bread slices. Spread each slice with avocado, top with asparagus ribbons and roasted tomatoes, and serve immediately.

GREEN TIP: Slice the tartine into smaller portions for an appetizer.

CALORIES (PER SERVING)	515
PROTEIN	15.6 g
TOTAL FAT	20.3 g
SATURATED FAT	3.6 g
CARBOHYDRATES	71.2 g
DIETARY FIBER	12.9 g
SUGARS	7.3 g
VITAMINS	C, K

QUICK COUSCOUS WITH SUMMER SQUASH AND TURNIP GREENS

 Serves 4-5

This dish goes from ingredients to table in 15 minutes. Not only is it a wonderful way to incorporate zucchini when it's overflowing from the garden, but it's so quick and easy, too. I like to serve it family-style from the skillet it was prepared in; it's rather pretty with almonds and fresh dill on top.

Prep: 5 mins | Cook: 15 mins

1 tablespoon olive oil
½ cup (75 g) onion, diced
1 medium zucchini, cubed
1 crookneck squash (or an extra zucchini), cubed
2 cups (80 g) turnip greens, chopped
½ teaspoon dried basil
¼ teaspoon dried thyme
3 cups (750 ml) vegetable broth
2 cups (360 g) couscous
¼ cup (40 g) almonds
sprigs of fresh dill
(See image, page 127, rear)

1 Heat the oil in a large skillet with a tight-fitting lid. Add the onion and sauté for 3 to 4 minutes. Add the zucchini, squash, and greens, along with the dried herbs, and cook for 5 to 7 minutes, stirring occasionally, until the squash is fork-tender and the greens have wilted.

2 Meanwhile, in a small pan, bring the broth to a boil. Add the couscous to the vegetables and stir to mix. Carefully and slowly, add the hot broth to the skillet, stir again, then cover and remove from the heat. Allow to steam for 5 to 6 minutes, until the couscous is tender and all the liquid has been absorbed, then uncover, sprinkle the almonds and dill over the top, and serve.

CALORIES (PER SERVING)	378
PROTEIN	14.5 g
TOTAL FAT	8.2 g
SATURATED FAT	1 g
CARBOHYDRATES	60.9 g
DIETARY FIBER	6.3 g
SUGARS	2.8 g
VITAMINS	A, B6

STUFFED BAKED SWEET POTATOES WITH BROCCOLI, SWISS CHARD, AND HUMMUS

 Serves 2 | gluten-free

Forget a white-fleshed baked potato with sour cream—this healthy version is ten times better for you and your taste buds! Thanks to the greens, it's loaded with vitamins A, C, and K.

Prep: 10 mins | Cook: 60 mins

2 sweet potatoes
2 cups (70 g) Swiss chard leaves
1 tablespoon olive oil
1 tablespoon minced fresh ginger
1 cup (90 g) broccoli, chopped
juice of ½ lime
⅔ cup hummus (see page 52; or use your favorite chickpea hummus)

1 Preheat the oven to 400°F (200°C). Skewer the potatoes with a fork several times and place in a suitable baking dish. Bake for an hour, or until fork-tender. Remove from the oven and allow to cool for 5 minutes before slicing carefully down the middle, keeping the potatoes intact. Score and mash the insides of the potatoes gently with a fork, keeping their shape.

2 Stack the chard leaves and roll them into a tight cigar. Slice thinly, so that you end up with long, thin ribbons of greens. Set aside.

3 In a medium saucepan, heat the oil and add the minced ginger, cooking for 1 to 2 minutes until fragrant. Add the broccoli and sauté for 2 minutes until bright green. Cover with a lid and steam in the pan for 3 to 5 minutes, or until fork-tender. Remove lid, add the chopped chard and lime juice, and cook uncovered for 2 to 3 minutes, until the leaves are wilted.

4 Pile the potatoes high with the chard, broccoli, and hummus. Serve with hot sauce on the side for those who like it spicy.

CALORIES (PER SERVING)	350
PROTEIN	10.3 g
TOTAL FAT	15.6 g
SATURATED FAT	2.3 g
CARBOHYDRATES	46.9 g
DIETARY FIBER	11.4 g
SUGARS	1.9 g
VITAMINS	A, C, K

CHICKPEA AND FENNEL CURRY ON A BED OF FRESH WATERCRESS

 Serves 4 / gluten-free

Fresh, peppery watercress fits right at home with a bowl of peanut curry.

Prep: 10 mins | Cook: 20 mins

1 tablespoon coconut oil

1 small onion, diced

1-inch (2.5-cm) piece fresh ginger, minced

2 tablespoons Thai red curry paste

1 bulb fennel, fronds removed, cored and sliced

1 x 15 oz (425 g) can chickpeas, drained and rinsed

1 x 14 oz (400 g) can coconut milk

3 tablespoons natural peanut butter

6–8 cups (210–280 g) watercress, roots and stems removed

sea salt

cooked rice, to serve

fresh cilantro, to serve

1 In a large skillet, heat the coconut oil. Add the onion and sauté for 3 to 4 minutes, then add the ginger and curry paste and stir while it cooks for another 1 to 2 minutes, until fragrant.

2 Add the fennel, chickpeas, and coconut milk. Increase the heat and bring the mixture to a boil. Reduce heat to low, cover, and simmer for 10 minutes.

3 Place the peanut butter in a bowl. Carefully ladle out a ½ cup (120 ml) of coconut milk from the pan and add it to the peanut butter, stirring until smooth. Add this to the curry and stir well. Simmer uncovered for 5 minutes until heated through, then season to taste with salt.

4 To serve, scoop a cup of cooked rice into each bowl, divide the watercress evenly between the bowls and ladle hot curry over the top. Garnish with fresh cilantro and enjoy.

CALORIES (PER SERVING)	499
PROTEIN	16.3 g
TOTAL FAT	35.2 g
SATURATED FAT	24.2 g
CARBOHYDRATES	33.9 g
DIETARY FIBER	10.8 g
SUGARS	3.1 g
VITAMINS	B6, C

FRENCH LENTILS WITH ASPARAGUS AND SHALLOTS

 Serves 3 / gluten-free

This dish makes for a light yet hearty main when served alongside a leafy salad and some crusty bread. If French lentils aren't available, brown or green lentils can be substituted.

Prep: 10 mins | Cook: 30 mins

1 cup (200 g) French lentils

3 cups (750 ml) water

2 tablespoons extra virgin olive oil

3 to 4 small shallots, skins removed and thinly sliced

juice of 1 lemon

1 bunch (about 12 oz (350 g)) asparagus, woody ends removed

sea salt and freshly ground black pepper

1 avocado, sliced, to serve

lemon wedges, to serve

1 Rinse the lentils well under running water. In a small pan, bring the lentils and water to a rolling boil, stir, reduce heat, and simmer for 25 to 30 minutes, or until the lentils are tender. Season the lentils with a few pinches of salt. Drain off any remaining liquid and set aside.

2 Meanwhile, heat the olive oil in a large skillet. Add the shallots and cook over medium-low heat for 15 minutes, stirring frequently.

3 Raise the heat to medium-high and add the lemon juice and asparagus. Cook for 5 to 7 minutes, until the asparagus brightens and is easily pierced with a fork. Add the cooked lentils to the pan, season to taste, and heat through.

4 Serve warm, topped with sliced avocado and lemon wedges.

CALORIES (PER SERVING)	348
PROTEIN	20.2 g
TOTAL FAT	10.3 g
SATURATED FAT	1.6 g
CARBOHYDRATES	46.7 g
DIETARY FIBER	22.7 g
SUGARS	4.3 g
VITAMINS	A, B6, C, K

DECONSTRUCTED SUSHI BOWL

Serves 2 / gluten-free

I love sushi, and I love making it at home, but sometimes I can't be bothered taking the time to roll it. Enter the Deconstructed Sushi Bowl—it's all the yummy stuff from a cucumber-avocado roll, in a bowl.

Prep: 45 mins | Cook: 12 to 15 mins

1 cup (200 g) short grain brown rice

1 sheet toasted nori

½ x 16 oz (454 g) pack extra-firm tofu

2 teaspoons olive oil

½ teaspoon powdered ginger

1 teaspoon garlic powder

⅛ teaspoon sea salt

⅛ teaspoon freshly ground black pepper

⅓ cucumber, seeded and chopped

1 ripe avocado, sliced

1 tablespoon toasted sesame seeds

pickled ginger, to serve

wasabi, to serve

tamari, to serve

(*See image, rear*)

1 Prepare the rice according to the packet directions. Slice the nori into thin matchstick-sized strips.

2 Preheat the oven to 375°F (190°C). To prepare the tofu, wrap it in a clean tea towel and gently press the water out of it, either by hand or by placing it on a plate and weighing it down with a cast-iron pan or a few books. After around 15 minutes, slice it into bite-sized cubes, toss in the olive oil, and sprinkle with powdered ginger, garlic powder, salt, and pepper. Spread out on a baking sheet lined with parchment paper and cook for 12 to 15 minutes, until browned.

3 Divide the rice between two bowls and pile on the cucumber, avocado, nori, and tofu. Sprinkle with toasted sesame seeds and serve with pickled ginger, wasabi, and tamari on the side.

CALORIES (PER SERVING)	638
PROTEIN	21 g
TOTAL FAT	25.1 g
SATURATED FAT	3.5 g
CARBOHYDRATES	86.9 g
DIETARY FIBER	14.3 g
SUGARS	4.6 g
VITAMINS	C, K

BUTTERNUT SQUASH AND MILLET SALAD BOWL WITH CHICKPEA CROUTONS

Serves 2 / gluten-free

Some salads deserve to be served as an entrée. All it takes is a big portion and lots of ingredients to make a meal of it. Wait until you taste the chickpea croutons—aside from the fresh greens, they might just be my favorite part!

Prep: 10 mins | Cook: 55 mins

1 cup (250 ml) water

½ cup (100 g) millet

2 cups (400 g) butternut squash, peeled and cubed

1 tablespoon coconut oil, melted

½ teaspoon smoked paprika

1 x 15 oz (425 g) can chickpeas, drained and rinsed

1 tablespoon olive oil

1 tablespoon tamari

½ teaspoon garlic powder

1 head radicchio

1 head butter lettuce (or Bibb lettuce)

sea salt

1 batch of Miso Tahini Dressing (page 110)

(See image, opposite, front)

1 Bring the water to a boil in a medium saucepan, add a pinch of salt and the millet, and stir. Cover the pot with a tight-fitting lid and simmer for 20 minutes over a low heat. Remove from the heat and fluff with a fork. All of the water should have been absorbed and the millet will be tender.

2 Meanwhile, preheat the oven to 425°F (220°C). Toss the butternut squash with the coconut oil and sprinkle with smoked paprika. Spread out in a glass baking dish and bake for 25 to 35 minutes, stirring halfway through, until tender and starting to brown. Remove from the oven and leave to cool.

3 Lower the oven temperature to 375°F (190°C). Toss the chickpeas in a bowl with the olive oil, tamari, and garlic powder, then spread out on a baking sheet lined with parchment. Cook in the oven for 15 to 20 minutes, stirring every 5 minutes, until browned and beginning to crisp up. Remove from the oven; the chickpeas will continue to crisp as they cool.

4 Chop or tear the radicchio and butter lettuce. Toss with the millet and dressing, then top with the roasted squash and chickpea croutons.

GREEN TIP: No butter or Bibb lettuce? No worries! Use whatever salad greens are fresh and in season: oak leaf, romaine, baby spinach, and even massaged kale would all be amazing.

CALORIES (PER SERVING)	668
PROTEIN	26.8 g
TOTAL FAT	19.5 g
SATURATED FAT	7.8 g
CARBOHYDRATES	101.9 g
DIETARY FIBER	23.7 g
SUGARS	9.1 g
VITAMINS	A, C

SWEET POTATO AND GREENS BURGER

Serves 4

These burgers are really tender and yummy, and a favorite with kids and adults alike. I usually make them with beet greens, but any leafy green will work well. They are a little too delicate to hold up over direct heat, but you could cook them on a well-oiled cast-iron pan on the barbecue.

Prep: 40 mins | Cook: 100 mins

1 large sweet potato

1 cup (170 g) cooked pinto beans (drained and rinsed, if canned)

1 cup (40 g) greens (beet greens, radish greens, turnip greens, chard, etc.), chopped

2 green onions, diced

½ cup (45 g) rolled oats

1½ teaspoons vegan Worcestershire sauce

1 teaspoon umeboshi vinegar

2 tablespoons tahini

3 tablespoons tamari

juice of 1 lemon

sea salt and freshly ground black pepper

4 burger buns, to serve

sprouts or fresh arugula, to serve

1 Preheat the oven to 400°F (200°C). Skewer the potato with a fork several times and place in a suitable dish. Bake for an hour, or until fork-tender. Remove from the oven and allow to cool for 5 minutes before peeling and mashing the potato in a large bowl.

2 Add the pinto beans to the bowl and mash them in too, then add the greens, onions, oats, Worcestershire sauce, umeboshi vinegar, and seasoning, and mix to combine. Refrigerate for 30 minutes.

3 Reheat the oven to 400°F (200°C). Form the mixture into four patties, place on a baking sheet, and cook for 20 minutes, then flip over and bake for another 15 minutes. If desired, you can then pan fry them for 2 to 3 minutes on each side.

4 Whisk together the tahini, tamari, lemon juice, and a pinch of sea salt until smooth. Thin out with a little water to the desired consistency, if necessary. Serve the burgers on the buns, topped with the lemon tahini sauce and sprouts or arugula.

CALORIES (PER SERVING)	356
PROTEIN	15.5 g
TOTAL FAT	7.3 g
SATURATED FAT	1.3 g
CARBOHYDRATES	60.4 g
DIETARY FIBER	11.9 g
SUGARS	8.2 g
VITAMINS	A

CREAMY SPINACH CURRY WITH TOFU PANEER

Serves 4 / gluten-free

This flavorful curry is a cinch to make, and the tofu does a great job of standing in for paneer, with its mild taste and texture. To spice things up a bit, increase the cayenne pepper and try adding 2 cups (about 30 g) of arugula to the mix.

Prep: 10 mins | Cook: 20 mins

1 lb (450 g) spinach

4 tablespoons vegetable oil

1 tablespoon cumin seeds

1 teaspoon ground cumin

1 teaspoon ground coriander

1 teaspoon turmeric

½ teaspoon cayenne pepper

2 teaspoons sea salt

1 x 28 oz (800 g) can whole tomatoes, puréed

½ x 12 oz (350 g) pack tofu, cut into 1-inch (2.5-cm) cubes

1 cup (250 ml) full-fat coconut milk

cooked brown basmati rice, to serve

1 Wash the spinach and trim the ends. Cut the stems in half and the leaves into 2-inch (5-cm) pieces. Set aside.

2 Heat the oil in a large pan. Add the cumin seeds and allow them to sizzle for 30 seconds. Add the rest of the spices, salt, tomatoes, and tofu. Stir, reduce heat to low, cover, and let simmer for 10 minutes.

3 Add the coconut milk and spinach stems, increase heat to medium, and continue to cook for another 5 to 6 minutes, until the stems are tender. Then add the spinach greens and cook for a final 3 minutes, until wilted. Serve alongside brown basmati rice.

GREEN TIP: This recipe calls for 1lb (450 g) spinach—most bunches of spinach at the grocery store are this size, so it makes shopping easy.

CALORIES (PER SERVING)	349
PROTEIN	9.9 g
TOTAL FAT	28.3 g
SATURATED FAT	14.2 g
CARBOHYDRATES	16.8 g
DIETARY FIBER	5.1 g
SUGARS	7 g
VITAMINS	A, C

COLLARD AND QUINOA "CABBAGE ROLLS"

Serves 4 / gluten-free

I can't say that traditional cabbage rolls were ever my cup of tea, but I love this collard and quinoa version. They are awesome on a cold winter's night.

Prep: 10 mins | Cook: 55 mins

8 large collard leaves
2 tablespoons olive oil
2 cloves garlic, minced
1¼ cups (210 g) quinoa
1 large carrot, diced
½ teaspoon dried basil
½ teaspoon dried oregano
2½ cups (625 ml) vegetable broth
1 small onion, diced
1 x 14 oz (400 g) can whole or diced tomatoes, puréed
¼ teaspoon chili flakes
pinch of sea salt
(See image, page 135, rear)

1 Prepare the collard leaves. Turn them over to expose their backs. Carefully run a sharp knife along the tough stem, removing most of it. Trim the remaining stem bottoms. Place the leaves in a pot of boiling water for 1 minute, then remove and place them in an iced water bath for 1 minute, blanching them. Pat them dry on a tea towel and set aside.

2 In a medium pan, heat 1 tablespoon of oil. Add the garlic and sauté for 1 to 2 minutes, stirring so that it doesn't burn. Add the quinoa, carrot, and herbs and mix to coat in the oil. Cook for another minute, then add the broth and bring to a boil. Reduce heat, cover, and simmer for 15 minutes, until all the liquid has been absorbed. Remove from heat and let sit for 5 minutes, then fluff with a fork.

3 Heat the remaining oil in a small pan. Add the onion and sauté until softened and translucent, about 5 minutes. Add the tomatoes, chili flakes, and salt and simmer over a medium-low heat for 10 minutes.

4 Preheat the oven to 350°F (180°C). Add half the tomato sauce to an 8 x 8-inch (20 x 20-cm) baking dish. Lay out a collard leaf and add about ⅓ cup of quinoa filling to just below the middle. Fold in the sides on top of the quinoa, then roll up like a burrito. Place seam-down in the baking dish. Repeat with the other collard leaves, then pour the remaining tomato sauce over the top. Bake for 25 minutes and serve.

CALORIES (PER SERVING)	318
PROTEIN	12.3 g
TOTAL FAT	11.1 g
SATURATED FAT	1.6 g
CARBOHYDRATES	43.8 g
DIETARY FIBER	7.5 g
SUGARS	5.7 g
VITAMINS	A, B6, C

ROMAINE TACOS WITH SOUTHWEST QUINOA

Serves 2 / gluten-free

Romaine leaves make the perfect taco shell—with their crisp leaves and crunchy middle rib, they are already shaped to be filled. This cumin-scented quinoa is the perfect filling, too.

Prep: 10 mins | Cook: 20 mins

1 cup (170 g) quinoa
1 cup (250 ml) water
1 cup (250 ml) vegetable broth
1 teaspoon cumin seeds
2 cups (300 g) sweet potato, peeled and cubed
1 cup (170 g) cooked black beans (drained and rinsed, if canned)
2 green onions, diced
¼ cup (10 g) cilantro, chopped
4–6 romaine leaves
avocado slices, to serve
salsa, to serve
lime wedges, to serve
(See image, opposite, front)

1 Combine the quinoa, water, broth, and cumin seeds in a medium pan and bring to a boil. Reduce the heat, cover, and simmer for 15 minutes, until all the liquid has been absorbed. Remove from the heat and let rest for 5 minutes. Fluff the quinoa with a fork.

2 Meanwhile, steam the sweet potato cubes until fork-tender, about 10 minutes. Add the sweet potato, beans, onions, and cilantro to the quinoa and stir to combine.

3 To serve, divide the mixture between the romaine taco shells and top with avocado, salsa, and a squeeze of fresh lime.

CALORIES (PER SERVING)	566
PROTEIN	23.3 g
TOTAL FAT	6.3 g
SATURATED FAT	0.9 g
CARBOHYDRATES	105.2 g
DIETARY FIBER	16.6 g
SUGARS	0.8 g
VITAMINS	A, C

SAMOSA BURRITOS WITH PEAS

Serves 4 / gluten-free option

Why make samosas when you can make samosa burritos and fill them with good-for-you green things? This is my kind of epicurean fusion. For a gluten-free option, use gluten-free or collard wraps.

Prep: 10 mins | Cook: 35 mins

3 cups (450 g) potato, peeled and chopped into 1-inch (2.5-cm) pieces

1 cup (130 g) carrot, diced

1⅓ cups (190 g) fresh or frozen green peas

2 tablespoons vegetable oil, plus extra for frying

1 tablespoon cumin seeds

1 tablespoon fenugreek seeds

1 teaspoon ground coriander

½ teaspoon amchoor powder (optional)

1 teaspoon sea salt

1 cup (150 g) onion, diced

1 cup (45 g) cilantro, chopped

4 tortillas (10-inch (25-cm))

mango chutney (optional), to serve

lime pickle (optional), to serve

1 Bring a large pan of salted water to a boil, add the potatoes, and boil for 10 minutes. With 4 minutes of cooking time remaining, add the carrots to the pan, and with 1 minute remaining, add the peas. Drain the vegetables into a colander.

2 In a medium skillet or frying pan, heat the oil. Add the cumin and fenugreek seeds and cook for 1 minute in the hot oil, then add the rest of the spices and the salt and stir. Add the onion and sauté for 3 to 4 minutes, until softened. Add the potatoes, peas, carrots, and cilantro to the spices and stir well, mashing gently with the back of the spatula. Cook the mixture for 5 to 6 minutes, until well cooked through, then remove from the heat and allow to cool until you can work with it, about 10 minutes.

3 Scoop a quarter of the potato mixture into a tortilla. Fold in the sides, and then roll up from the bottom, tucking in the edges. Lay seam-down so it doesn't unroll. Repeat with the remaining tortillas.

4 Wipe out the frying pan with a paper towel and heat 1 teaspoon of vegetable oil. Place the burritos in the pan, seam-down, and cook for 2 minutes. Flip them over and sear the tops for 2 minutes, until crispy and golden brown on both sides. Serve with the chutney and pickle, if desired.

CALORIES (PER SERVING)	303
PROTEIN	7.9 g
TOTAL FAT	10.7 g
SATURATED FAT	2 g
CARBOHYDRATES	46.1 g
DIETARY FIBER	9.2 g
SUGARS	6.9 g
VITAMINS	A, B6, C

KALE AND KABOCHA ENCHILADAS VERDE

 Serves 4 | gluten-free option

I've never met a vegan enchilada I didn't like, and these are no exception. For a gluten-free option, use gluten-free or collard wraps.

Prep: 15 mins | Cook: 90 mins

1 small kabocha squash

4 teaspoons coconut oil

2 cups (140 g) kale leaves, stems removed

1 cup (150 g) onion, diced

1 cup (170 g) cooked black beans (drained and rinsed, if canned)

1 teaspoon ground cumin

sea salt

8 whole wheat tortillas (6-inch)

¼ cup vegan cheese shreds (optional)

FOR THE ENCHILADA VERDE SAUCE

3 cups (450 g) fresh tomatillos

½ cup (75 g) onion, diced

2 cups (500 ml) vegetable broth

1 jalapeño pepper, seeds and membranes removed, chopped

¼ cup (10 g) fresh cilantro, finely chopped

CALORIES (PER SERVING)	521
PROTEIN	20.4 g
TOTAL FAT	10 g
SATURATED FAT	4.3 g
CARBOHYDRATES	92.1 g
DIETARY FIBER	17.3 g
SUGARS	11.7 g
VITAMINS	A, B6, C

1 Preheat the oven to 350°F (180°C). Slice the squash in half from top to bottom. Scoop out the seeds and stringy bits, then place the halves, cut-side up, in a baking dish filled with ¼ inch (0.5-cm) water. Add 1 teaspoon coconut oil to the seed cavity of each half and bake until fork-tender, about 45 minutes. Set aside to cool, then remove the flesh and cube. Stack the kale leaves and slice them into ribbons.

2 Heat the remaining oil in a large pan. Sauté the onions until translucent. Add the kale, black beans, squash, and cumin. Continue to cook for 5 minutes, until the kale is cooked down and tender, then season to taste with salt and remove from the heat to cool.

3 For the sauce, peel and quarter the tomatillos. Put the tomatillos, onion, and broth in a medium saucepan and simmer, covered, for 15 minutes, until the tomatillos are tender. Remove the tomatillos and most of the onion with a slotted spoon and purée them in a blender or food processor. Return the purée to the pot of broth, add the jalapeño and cilantro, increase the heat to bring the mixture to a boil, then cook until the sauce has thickened and reduced to about 2 cups.

4 Reheat the oven to 350°F (180°C). Spoon ½ cup of the enchilada sauce into a 9 x 13-inch (23 x 33-cm) baking dish. Add ½ cup of the kale and kabocha mixture to a tortilla and roll it up. Place it seam-down in the dish and repeat with the remaining tortillas. Spoon the rest of the enchilada sauce over the rolled tortillas. If using, sprinkle with cheese shreds. Place in the oven and bake for 25 minutes.

GREEN TIP: Save time by cubing the squash and steaming it for 15 minutes, or until tender. And instead of making your own sauce, use a 16 oz jar of salsa verde.

RAPINI À LA PUTTANESCA

Serves 4 / gluten-free

Make a change on pasta night by serving a bold sauce over greens instead. Each serving is made up of a half bunch of rapini, so this dish is a triple treat—healthy, green, and filling.

Prep: 10 mins | Cook: 30 mins

3 tablespoons olive oil

1 onion, finely diced

1 x 28 oz (800 g) can whole or diced tomatoes, puréed

¼ cup (60 ml) dry white wine

½ cup (50 g) kalamata olives, chopped

⅓ cup (20 g) sundried tomatoes in oil, sliced

2 tablespoons capers

2 bunches rapini

2 cloves garlic, peeled and crushed

pinch of dried chili flakes (optional)

¾ cup (190 ml) vegetable broth

sea salt and freshly ground black pepper

1 In a large pan, heat 1 tablespoon of olive oil, add the onions and sauté for 5 minutes, until translucent. Add the tomatoes and wine and simmer while stirring for 2 minutes. Add the olives, sundried tomatoes, and capers. Reduce heat, and cook at just below a simmer for 15 to 20 minutes, until the sauce has thickened. Season to taste.

2 Meanwhile, wash the rapini and trim the bottom half of the stems. Shake or spin off the excess water. Heat the remaining olive oil in a large skillet with a lid. Add the garlic and chili flakes and cook for 2 to 3 minutes. Then add the rapini, turning it with tongs and adding more as it wilts and creates more room in the pan. Once all the rapini is in the pan, sprinkle with a generous pinch of sea salt. Add the broth and increase the heat, bringing the liquid to a simmer. Cover the pan and cook the greens for 6 to 8 minutes, until tender and cooked through.

3 To serve, arrange the greens on a large serving platter or individual plates. Try to leave as much of the cooking liquid behind in the pan as possible. Spoon the tomato sauce over the top and serve.

CALORIES (PER SERVING)	204
PROTEIN	5.2 g
TOTAL FAT	12.9 g
SATURATED FAT	1.9 g
CARBOHYDRATES	17.5 g
DIETARY FIBER	3.8 g
SUGARS	7.6 g
VITAMINS	A, B6, C

SPINACH AND MUSHROOM GALETTE

 Serves 6

A galette is a rustic, free-form French pie. They can be sweet, but a savory galette is a great dish to have in your repertoire. Don't let the homemade pastry intimidate you—it's so easy, and since rustic is the name of the game, it needn't be perfect either.

Prep: 30 mins | Cook: 30 mins

1 cup (125 g) whole wheat flour
¼ cup (30 g) all-purpose flour
¼ cup (60 ml) coconut oil
½ cup (125 ml) iced water
2 portobello mushrooms
2 tablespoons, plus
1½ teaspoons olive oil
1 large clove garlic, minced
6–8 cremini mushrooms
1 teaspoon fresh thyme leaves
4 cups (120 g) spinach
1 cup (240 g) firm tofu
3 teaspoons lemon juice
1 teaspoon nutritional yeast
¼ teaspoon garlic powder
sea salt and freshly ground
black pepper

CALORIES (PER SERVING)	266
PROTEIN	7.5 g
TOTAL FAT	17.1 g
SATURATED FAT	9.1 g
CARBOHYDRATES	22.8 g
DIETARY FIBER	1.9 g
SUGARS	0.9 g
VITAMINS	A

1 Make the pastry. In a large bowl, mix together the flours and ½ teaspoon salt. Using a pastry cutter or your fingers, work the coconut oil into the flour, leaving small lumps. Sprinkle over the water and work until the dough just comes together. Roll into a ball, wrap in plastic wrap, and refrigerate for 20 minutes.

2 Remove the stems and black gills from the portobello mushrooms and slice into long pieces, ½ inch (1-cm) thick. Heat 2 tablespoons oil in a large pan over medium heat, add the garlic, and sauté until fragrant, about 1 minute. Add all the mushrooms and a generous pinch of sea salt and cook, stirring occasionally, for 15 to 20 minutes, until the mushrooms release their juices and the juices evaporate. Remove the pan from the heat, sprinkle with thyme, and set aside.

3 Meanwhile, steam the spinach lightly, for 30 seconds to 1 minute, until partially wilted but still holding a little structure. Leave to cool.

4 Place the tofu, lemon juice, 1½ teaspoons olive oil, nutritional yeast, and garlic powder in a food processor, and process until fairly smooth. Season to taste with salt and pepper, then transfer to a bowl. Add the spinach and fold in by hand.

5 Preheat the oven to 400°F (200°C). On a piece of parchment paper, roll out the pastry to a 12-inch (30-cm) round. Transfer the pastry and parchment onto a baking sheet and spread the spinach-tofu mixture over, leaving a 2-inch (5-cm) border all around the perimeter. Top with the sautéed mushrooms, again leaving a border. Gently fold the extra pastry up and onto the toppings, pleating as you move around the outside.

6 Bake in the oven for 30 to 35 minutes, until the edges of the pastry are golden brown. Remove from the oven and let sit for 5 minutes before slicing and serving.

MOROCCAN TAGINE WITH APRICOT COUSCOUS

Serves 4 | gluten-free option

Tagines are Moroccan stews named for the gorgeous clay pots in which they're traditionally cooked. I don't own one, but I didn't let that hold me back from creating this flavorful dish that is loaded with green veggies and accented with cinnamon and raisins. For a gluten-free option, serve with millet in place of couscous.

Prep: 15 mins | Cook: 25 mins

1 tablespoon coconut oil

1 medium onion, diced

1-inch (2.5-cm) piece fresh ginger, minced

1 tablespoon harissa

1 cinnamon stick

1 teaspoon cumin seeds

½ teaspoon smoked paprika

1 x 14 oz (400 g) can diced tomatoes

⅔ cup (110 g) canned chickpeas, drained and rinsed

1 carrot, chopped

1 zucchini, chopped

1 cup (90 g) broccoli, chopped

1 cup (150 g) green beans, chopped

1 rib celery, chopped

⅓ cup (50 g) peas

⅓ cup (50 g) raisins

1½ cups (375 ml) water

1 cup (180 g) couscous

6 unsulfured apricots, cut into small pieces

¼ teaspoon cinnamon

sea salt

handful of fresh cilantro, chopped, to serve

2 tablespoons sliced almonds, to serve

1 Heat the oil over medium-high heat in a large skillet with a tight-fitting lid. Add the onion, ginger, and harissa and cook while stirring for 2 to 3 minutes. Add the cinnamon stick, cumin seeds, paprika, and tomatoes. Stir well and bring to a boil, then add the chickpeas, vegetables, and raisins and stir.

2 Reduce heat to low, then cover and leave things to simmer for 15 minutes, or until the vegetables are tender. Season to taste with salt.

3 Meanwhile, bring the water to a boil in a small pan. Stir in the couscous, apricots, and cinnamon, then immediately remove from heat, cover, and let sit for 5 to 6 minutes. Fluff with a fork.

4 Divide the apricot couscous between four plates and top with the tagine, fresh cilantro, and sliced almonds.

CALORIES (PER SERVING)	426
PROTEIN	13.4 g
TOTAL FAT	6.9 g
SATURATED FAT	3.2 g
CARBOHYDRATES	80.6 g
DIETARY FIBER	12.1 g
SUGARS	21.6 g
VITAMINS	A, B6, C

GREEN CAKES AND DESSERTS

CHOCOLATE-DIPPED KALE CHIPS

 Serves 6 / gluten-free

Instead of the usual savory kale chips, mix things up with a raw chocolate coating.

Prep: 15 mins | Cook: 45 to 60 mins

1 bunch kale (about 6½ cups/450 g)

5 tablespoons coconut oil, melted

1 teaspoon pure vanilla extract

3 tablespoons agave nectar

¼ cup (30 g), plus 2 tablespoons raw cacao powder

2 tablespoons chia seeds

3 tablespoons shredded unsweetened coconut

(*See image, opposite, rear*)

1 Preheat the oven to 225°F (110°C). Line two cookie sheets with parchment paper.

2 Wash the kale and, using a sharp knife, cut out the tough rib. Stack the leaves and cut into large chip-sized pieces. Pat dry and set aside.

3 In a large bowl, combine the coconut oil, vanilla, and agave. Whisk in the cacao powder, making sure there are no lumps. Fold in the chia seeds and the coconut.

4 Add the kale to the chocolate mixture and toss well so that all the leaves are coated. Spread the kale out on the two cookie sheets, ensuring it is in a single layer.

5 Bake for 45 to 60 minutes with the oven door open a crack. Gently rearrange the kale after 30 minutes of cooking time and rotate the cookie sheets to ensure even baking. Keep a close eye on them to ensure they don't burn. Remove from the oven and allow to cool before serving.

CALORIES (PER SERVING)	219
PROTEIN	4.6 g
TOTAL FAT	13.9 g
SATURATED FAT	11.2 g
CARBOHYDRATES	21.5 g
DIETARY FIBER	6.5 g
SUGARS	5.6 g
VITAMINS	A, C, K

SECRET INGREDIENT BROWNIES

 *Makes 16*

Moist, dense, chewy brownies made with . . . spinach!

Prep: 10 mins | Cook: 35 mins

3 cups (90 g) loosely-packed spinach leaves

¾ cup (190 ml) non-dairy milk

1¼ cups (250 g) unrefined cane sugar

2 tablespoons coconut oil, melted

1⅓ cups (165 g) whole wheat flour

½ cup (60 g) cocoa powder

1 teaspoon baking powder

¼ teaspoon salt

½ cup (75 g) non-dairy chocolate chips

(*See image, front*)

1 Preheat the oven to 350°F (180°C). Spray or grease an 8 x 8-inch (20 x 20-cm) baking pan.

2 Combine the spinach and milk in a food processor and blend until smooth. Empty into a bowl and whisk in the sugar and coconut oil.

3 In a separate bowl, sift together the flour, cocoa powder, baking powder, and salt. Add this to the wet ingredients, stirring until you have a thick batter. Fold in the chocolate chips.

4 Spread the batter into the prepared pan and bake for 35 minutes, or until a toothpick inserted into the edge of a brownie comes out clean; it's fine if it's still slightly moist in the center. Leave to cool, then serve.

CALORIES (PER SERVING)	167
PROTEIN	2.3 g
TOTAL FAT	6.1 g
SATURATED FAT	4.9 g
CARBOHYDRATES	29.1 g
DIETARY FIBER	1.5 g
SUGARS	18.6 g
VITAMINS	A, K

CHOCOLATE HAZELNUT AVOCADO TORTE

 Serves 10 / gluten-free

A beautiful raw torte that is rich, chocolatey, and full of heart-healthy fats from the hazelnuts and avocado.

Prep: 20 mins | Cook: 15 mins

1 cup (150 g), plus 1 tablespoon hazelnuts

1 cup (180 g) medjool dates, pitted

¼ cup (30 g), plus 2 tablespoons cocoa powder

2 large or 3 small avocados

pinch of sea salt

3 tablespoons maple syrup

¼ cup (35 g) non-dairy chocolate chips

1 Preheat the oven to 300°F (150°C).

2 Place 1 cup (150 g) hazelnuts on a baking sheet and toast them in the oven for 10 minutes. Let them cool, then place inside a clean tea towel folded over onto itself and rub the skins off.

3 Place the nuts in a food processor and pulse them into a coarse meal. Add the dates and 2 tablespoons of cocoa powder and process until the mixture reaches a sticky, crumbly texture. When pinched between two fingers it should stick together—if it doesn't it's too dry, so add a tablespoon of water and try again. Press the mixture down into a 9-inch (23-cm) tart pan with a removable base. (A springform pan or even a pie plate could be used here, although the presentation won't be quite as impressive.)

4 Prepare the filling by placing the remaining cocoa powder, avocado flesh, salt, and syrup in a food processor and process until smooth. Spoon the chocolate avocado filling into the crust and smooth with a spatula or the back of a spoon.

5 Melt the chocolate chips in a double boiler or in the microwave and drizzle on top. Chop the remaining tablespoon of hazelnuts and sprinkle on top. Refrigerate for 1 hour, or until ready to serve.

CALORIES (PER SERVING)	220
PROTEIN	3.4 g
TOTAL FAT	13.9 g
SATURATED FAT	2.8 g
CARBOHYDRATES	26.1 g
DIETARY FIBER	5.7 g
SUGARS	17.4 g
VITAMINS	E, K

SPINACH GINGER COOKIES

Makes 24

This recipe is a spin on the popular Molasses and Ginger Cookies sold in my bakeshop, with a dose of greens, of course. The spinach purée adds moisture, making for a more tender cookie. Kale works really well too if you are out of spinach.

Prep: 10 mins | Cook: 15 mins

1 cup (125 g) spelt or whole wheat flour

1 cup (125 g) all-purpose flour

½ cup (100 g) unrefined cane sugar, plus 2 tablespoons for rolling

1 tablespoon ground ginger

½ teaspoon cinnamon

pinch of ground cloves

1 teaspoon baking powder

½ teaspoon baking soda

½ teaspoon sea salt

1 cup (30 g) spinach, leaves and stems

¼ cup (60 ml) water

¼ cup (60 ml) canola oil

¼ cup (60 ml) molasses

(*See image, opposite, front*)

1 Preheat the oven to 375°F (190°C). Line a baking sheet with parchment paper.

2 In a large bowl, sift together the flours, sugar, spices, baking powder, baking soda, and salt and stir to combine.

3 Place the spinach, water, and oil in a food processor and blend to a purée. Stir in the molasses. Add the wet ingredients to the dry ingredients and mix well.

4 Scoop the cookie dough out by the tablespoon and roll into balls with damp hands. Roll the balls in the cane sugar and then flatten them with the bottom of a cup or your hand and lay on the baking sheet. Bake for 13 to 15 minutes, until the edges of the cookies are firm. Cool on the baking sheet for 5 minutes before transferring to a wire rack to finish cooling.

CALORIES (PER SERVING)	91
PROTEIN	1.3 g
TOTAL FAT	2.4 g
SATURATED FAT	0 g
CARBOHYDRATES	16.8 g
DIETARY FIBER	0.8 g
SUGARS	8.2 g
VITAMINS	A

ZUCCHINI OATMEAL COOKIES

Makes 16–20

These were inspired by a healthy breakfast cookie I baked for my one-year-old son. For my palate they needed sugar and a little more spice, and voilà—these zucchini cookies were born.

Prep: 10 mins | Cook: 18 mins

1 tablespoon chia seeds
4 tablespoons water
2 tablespoons vegan butter
1 cup (200 g) brown sugar
1 cup (125 g) whole wheat flour
1 teaspoon baking powder
½ teaspoon cinnamon
¼ teaspoon nutmeg
1⅓ cups (120 g) rolled oats
1 cup (120 g) grated zucchini
¼ cup (40 g) raisins (optional)
(See image, rear)

1 Preheat the oven to 375°F (190°C). Line a baking sheet with parchment paper.

2 Mix the chia seeds with 3 tablespoons water and leave to rest for 5 minutes until it becomes a gel.

3 In a bowl, cream together the butter and sugar. Add the chia gel and the remaining tablespoon of water and mix well.

4 Add the flour, baking powder, cinnamon, and nutmeg and mix well. Stir in the oats. Fold in the zucchini and raisins, if using.

5 Drop giant spoonfuls onto the baking sheet and flatten just a little. Bake for 16 to 18 minutes, or until the cookies have browned slightly on top and no longer look "wet." Transfer to a wire rack to cool.

CALORIES (PER SERVING)	125
PROTEIN	2 g
TOTAL FAT	2.1 g
SATURATED FAT	0 g
CARBOHYDRATES	25.3 g
DIETARY FIBER	1.3 g
SUGARS	13.7 g
VITAMINS	C

AVOCADO AND KIWI FROSTED BIRTHDAY CAKE

 Serves 8

This is a simple little cake that I baked for my son's first birthday. It is absolutely delicious—although he was far more interested in the kiwi fruit topping!

Prep: 10 mins | Cook: 40 mins

¾ cup (190 ml) almond milk

1 teaspoon apple cider vinegar

⅓ cup (85 ml) vegetable or canola oil

⅔ cup (170 ml) maple syrup

1⅔ cups (210 g) all-purpose flour

1 teaspoon baking powder

½ teaspoon baking soda

¼ teaspoon fine sea salt

FOR THE FROSTING

2 large ripe avocados

juice of ½ lime

2 tablespoons agave nectar

2 kiwis, peeled and sliced

1 Preheat the oven to 325°F (160°C). Lightly grease and flour two 6-inch (15-cm) cake pans and set aside.

2 Whisk together the almond milk and vinegar and leave to curdle for a minute or two. Then add the oil and maple syrup and stir to combine.

3 Sift in the dry ingredients and whisk until incorporated and no lumps remain.

4 Divide the batter between the cake pans and place them in the oven to bake for 35 to 40 minutes, or until a toothpick inserted into the cakes comes out clean. Remove from the oven and leave to cool.

5 For the frosting, scoop out the flesh of the avocados and place in a food processor with the lime juice and agave. Process until smooth and whipped up, stopping to scrape down the sides of the bowl as needed. Taste as you go and add more agave until you achieve the desired sweetness.

6 Remove the cooled cakes from the cake pans. Spread half of the frosting onto one of the cakes, then place the other cake on top and top with the remaining frosting and the kiwi slices. The lime juice will help to preserve the green color of the frosting, but not for too long, so it's best to make the frosting and assemble the cake just before you intend to serve it.

CALORIES (PER SERVING)	421
PROTEIN	4.4 g
TOTAL FAT	24.7 g
SATURATED FAT	7.5 g
CARBOHYDRATES	49.2 g
DIETARY FIBER	5.3 g
SUGARS	21.1 g
VITAMINS	C, K

COFFEE CAKE WITH GREEN GODDESS GRANOLA CRUMBLE

 Serves 9

This cake is like your favorite muffin with crumble topping, so it's guaranteed to disappear in no time. It's also the perfect way to use up that last little bit of granola.

Prep: 10 mins | Cook: 25 mins

1½ cups (185 g) whole wheat or spelt flour

½ cup (100 g) unrefined cane sugar

1½ teaspoons baking powder

1 teaspoon cinnamon

¼ teaspoon salt

¾ cup (190 ml) almond milk

¼ cup (60 ml) vegetable oil

FOR THE TOPPING

1 cup (100 g) Green Goddess Granola (page 28)

⅓ cup (65 g) brown sugar

2 tablespoons whole wheat flour

2 tablespoons vegan butter

1 Preheat the oven to 400°F (200°C). Lightly grease an 8 x 8-inch (20 x 20-cm) cake pan.

2 Mix together the dry ingredients. Add the milk and oil and stir to make a thick batter. Spread into the prepared pan.

3 Mix together the topping ingredients until a sandy texture is reached. Distribute on top of the batter and press down lightly.

4 Bake for 20 to 25 minutes, or until a toothpick inserted into the cake comes out clean. Allow to cool for 10 to 15 minutes, then slice and serve.

CALORIES (PER SERVING)	219
PROTEIN	2.6 g
TOTAL FAT	11 g
SATURATED FAT	5.5 g
CARBOHYDRATES	28.7 g
DIETARY FIBER	1.2 g
SUGARS	11.8 g
VITAMINS	A

LEMON AND PARSLEY OLIVE OIL CAKE

Serves 8–10

This cake is rich in flavor yet deliciously light. It's bursting with lemon and beautiful flecks of parsley throughout.

Prep: 10 mins | Cook: 50 mins

2 cups (250 g) all-purpose flour

½ teaspoon baking soda

1 teaspoon baking powder

¼ teaspoon salt

1 cup (200 g) unrefined cane sugar

¼ cup (60 ml) plain non-dairy yogurt

½ cup (125 ml) olive oil

1 tablespoon lemon zest

¼ cup (60 ml) fresh lemon juice

¼ cup (60 ml) water

⅔ cup (20 g) flat-leaf parsley, stems removed and finely chopped

powdered sugar, for dusting

(See image, rear)

1 Preheat the oven to 350°F (180°C). Lightly grease and flour a 9-inch (23-cm) cake pan.

2 Sift the flour, baking soda, baking powder, and salt into a bowl and mix to combine. Set aside.

3 In a separate bowl, mix together the sugar, yogurt, and olive oil until blended and light. Add the lemon zest, juice, and water and mix well.

4 Make a well in the middle of the dry ingredients and add the wet ingredients. Mix gently to incorporate. Fold in the parsley.

5 Pour into the prepared cake pan and bake for 45 to 50 minutes, or until a toothpick inserted into the cake comes out clean. Allow the cake to cool for at least 30 minutes before removing from the pan. Invert onto a plate, dust with powdered sugar, and serve.

CALORIES (PER SERVING)	289
PROTEIN	3.4 g
TOTAL FAT	11.8 g
SATURATED FAT	1.7 g
CARBOHYDRATES	44.5 g
DIETARY FIBER	1.1 g
SUGARS	22.6 g
VITAMINS	C

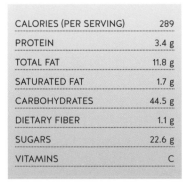

TRIPLE CHOCOLATE BEET GREENS CAKE

 Serves 10–12

This cake is so chocolatey and delicious—it's one of those that keeps you reaching for just one more little sliver, until suddenly you find you've eaten the whole thing.

Prep: 15 mins | Cook: 45 mins

1 bunch of beets (4 small beets, plus 2 cups (80 g) of greens)

½ cup (125 ml) vegetable oil

1 cup (200 g) brown sugar

⅓ cup (65 g) unrefined cane sugar

1 teaspoon pure vanilla extract

½ cup (75 g) non-dairy chocolate chips

1⅔ cups (210 g) all-purpose flour

¼ cup (30 g) cocoa powder

2 teaspoons baking powder

¼ teaspoon salt

FOR THE GANACHE

½ cup (75 g) non-dairy chocolate chips

2 tablespoons coconut oil

(See image, opposite, front)

1 Preheat the oven to 350°F (180°C). Lightly grease a bundt pan and "flour" with 1 to 2 teaspoons of cocoa powder.

2 Trim the beets of roots and stems. Wash and chop into 1-inch (2.5-cm) pieces. Chop the greens. Steam the beets for 10–15 minutes until fork-tender, then add the greens and continue steaming for another 5 minutes. Transfer to a food processor and purée until smooth, adding a tablespoon of water if needed. You should be left with around 1⅓ cups (330 ml) of purée.

3 In a large mixing bowl, cream together the oil, sugars, and vanilla. Melt the chocolate chips in a double boiler or in the microwave. Add the melted chocolate to the sugar, followed by the beet purée, and mix well.

4 Sift together the flour, cocoa powder, baking powder, and salt. Add this to the wet ingredients and mix gently until no clumps remain. Pour the batter into the prepared bundt pan and bake for 45 minutes, or until a toothpick inserted into the cake comes out clean. Cool for 15 minutes in the pan, then invert onto a cooling rack to continue cooling.

5 For the ganache, melt the chocolate chips with the oil until smooth. Glaze the top of the cake with the ganache and serve.

CALORIES (PER SERVING)	344
PROTEIN	3.8 g
TOTAL FAT	15.8 g
SATURATED FAT	6.1 g
CARBOHYDRATES	50.9 g
DIETARY FIBER	2.1 g
SUGARS	32.4 g
VITAMINS	A, K

ZUCCHINI CHOCOLATE CAKE

 Serves 8–10

Zucchini is an ideal vegetable for baking because of its mellow flavor, natural sweetness, and high moisture content. No one will ever guess this majorly rich chocolate cake is full of vegetables unless you tell them. It is so sweet on its own that it requires no icing—a little dusting of powdered sugar is just the right finish. You and your guests will love it!

Prep: 10 mins | Cook: 60 mins

1 cup (125 g) all-purpose flour
1 cup (200 g) unrefined cane sugar
½ cup (60 g) cocoa powder
1 teaspoon baking powder
1 teaspoon baking soda
½ teaspoon cinnamon
¼ teaspoon sea salt
⅔ cup (170 ml) vegetable oil
½ cup (125 ml) almond milk
1½ cups (180 g) grated zucchini
powdered sugar, for dusting

1 Preheat the oven to 350°F (180°C). Lightly grease a 6- or 8-inch (15- or 20-cm) cake pan.

2 Combine the flour, sugar, cocoa powder, baking powder, baking soda, cinnamon, and salt in a large bowl and stir.

3 Mix the oil and milk in another bowl and add to the dry ingredients. Stir until you have a thick batter. Then fold in the zucchini.

4 Pour the batter into the pan and bake for 50 to 60 minutes, or until a toothpick inserted into the cake comes out clean.

5 Allow the cake to cool before removing from the pan, dusting with powdered sugar, and slicing.

CALORIES (PER SERVING)	340
PROTEIN	2.8 g
TOTAL FAT	22.2 g
SATURATED FAT	6.8 g
CARBOHYDRATES	37.2 g
DIETARY FIBER	2.4 g
SUGARS	23.1 g
VITAMINS	C

STRAWBERRY, KIWI, AND CUCUMBER SALAD WITH COCONUT WHIPPED CREAM

 Serves 4 / gluten-free

This fruit (and vegetable) salad is the perfect dessert for when it's just too hot for baking. Cucumber is especially hydrating, and this salad is way more fun than drinking a glass of water, in my humble opinion.

Prep: 15 mins

2 cups (300 g) strawberries

3 kiwis

½ cucumber

FOR THE COCONUT WHIPPED CREAM

1 can (400 ml) full-fat coconut milk

3 tablespoons powdered sugar

(*See image, opposite, rear*)

1 Slice the strawberries, peel and slice the kiwis, and peel, deseed, and slice the cucumber. Combine in a bowl and toss.

2 For the coconut whipped cream, refrigerate the can of coconut milk overnight, or for at least 6 hours. Open the can, being mindful not to shake it. Scoop out the thick cream (which will have separated to the top) into a chilled metal bowl. Leave the coconut water aside (save it for a Cherry-Kale Quencher Smoothie, page 24). Sift the sugar into the bowl, then using an electric beater, whip the coconut cream until it forms peaks. Use immediately or return to the fridge until ready to use. You may need to briefly re-whip it before serving.

3 Divide the fruit into parfait glasses and serve with a dollop of coconut whipped cream.

CALORIES (PER SERVING)	290
PROTEIN	3 g
TOTAL FAT	20.9 g
SATURATED FAT	18.6 g
CARBOHYDRATES	24.6 g
DIETARY FIBER	7.5 g
SUGARS	16.2 g
VITAMINS	B6, C

SWEET MASSAGED KALE AND FRUIT SALAD WITH RAW CHOCOLATE SAUCE

 Serves 8–10 | gluten-free

Here is an easy and delicious way to get your greens for dessert. I love massaged kale salads, and with a drizzle of raw chocolate sauce it feels a bit like salad fondue!

Prep: 10 mins

3 cups (210 g) kale
1 teaspoon maple syrup
1 cup (125 g) raspberries
1 cup (145 g) blueberries
1 firm but ripe banana, sliced

FOR THE RAW CHOCOLATE SAUCE
¼ cup (60 ml) coconut oil, melted
¼ cup (30 g) cacao powder
3 tablespoons maple syrup
(*See image, front*)

1 Remove the stems and middle ribs from the kale leaves. Stack them and roll into a cigar, then slice as thinly as possible.

2 Drizzle the maple syrup over the kale and massage until the leaves begin to soften. Divide between individual plates and top with the fruit.

3 For the raw chocolate sauce, combine all ingredients together to make a smooth sauce. Drizzle over the kale leaves and fruit and serve.

CALORIES (PER SERVING)	214
PROTEIN	3.1 g
TOTAL FAT	12.4 g
SATURATED FAT	10.2 g
CARBOHYDRATES	28.7 g
DIETARY FIBER	5.4 g
SUGARS	14.7 g
VITAMINS	A, B6, C

VANILLA MINT CHEESECAKE

 Serves 8–10 | gluten-free

Chocolate and mint are a delicious pairing, but vanilla and mint are equally amazing, and this gorgeous raw cheesecake can attest to it. This can be made as a cake or as mini cheesecake bars. I like to keep the bars in the freezer and enjoy them frozen as a cool treat.

Prep: 10 mins | Chill: 120 mins

1 cup (170 g) almonds

pinch of sea salt

1 cup (180 g) dates

1½ cups (250 g) raw cashews, soaked for 4 to 6 hours

¼ cup (60 ml) agave nectar

2 tablespoons coconut oil, melted

2 tablespoons lemon juice

1 teaspoon pure vanilla extract

½ cup (15 g) spinach

1 tablespoon fresh mint

1. Place the almonds and salt in a food processor and pulse until they're ground to a coarse flour. Add the dates and blend until a sticky dough forms. Press into a 6-inch (15-cm) springform pan, or an 8 x 8-inch (20 x 20-cm) brownie pan if making cheesecake bars. Chill in the freezer while the filling is prepared.

2. Drain and rinse the cashews. Place them in a food processor along with the agave, coconut oil, lemon juice, and vanilla. Process until smooth. Pour three-quarters of the mixture into the chilled crust and spread out with a spatula.

3. To the last quarter of the mixture in the food processor, add the spinach and mint and blend until smooth. Top the vanilla filling with this mix, and again spread it out to the edges with a spatula. Or, if you're feeling adventurous, add the blend to the cheesecake a big spoonful at a time, then use a toothpick or chopstick to swirl it around and achieve a marbled effect.

4. Return the cheesecake to the freezer and chill for at least 2 hours. Slice while frozen and then allow to thaw in the refrigerator for an hour before serving, or serve straight from the freezer if you prefer a frozen treat.

CALORIES (PER SERVING)	296
PROTEIN	6.3 g
TOTAL FAT	19 g
SATURATED FAT	5.1 g
CARBOHYDRATES	30 g
DIETARY FIBER	4 g
SUGARS	19.1 g
VITAMINS	E

CELERY AND GRAPEFRUIT GRANITA

 Serves 4 / gluten-free

A refreshing and palate-cleansing dessert. The celery and grapefruit are a perfect match in this frozen treat.

Prep: 10 mins | Chill: 180 mins

2 cups (200 g) celery
1 ruby red grapefruit, peeled
¼ cup (60 ml) dandelion-infused simple syrup (page 173)
fresh raspberries, to serve
(*See image, opposite, rear*)

1 Chop the celery and grapefruit into bite-sized pieces, and place on a plate in the freezer for 1 hour.

2 Put the frozen vegetables into a food processor with the syrup and blend until smooth. Pour the contents into a glass baking dish and return to the freezer for 2 hours, taking it out every half hour or so to rake the mixture with a fork.

3 Divide between serving dishes and top with fresh raspberries.

CALORIES (PER SERVING)	58
PROTEIN	0.5 g
TOTAL FAT	0.1 g
SATURATED FAT	0 g
CARBOHYDRATES	14.6 g
DIETARY FIBER	1 g
SUGARS	13.6 g
VITAMINS	A, C

CHOCOLATE AVOCADO POPS

Serves 6–10 / gluten-free

These are a great summer treat and much healthier than the factory-made fudge pops. For the young and the young at heart.

Prep: 20 mins | Chill: 60 mins

8 medjool dates
⅔ cup (170 ml) warm water
2 avocados
⅔ cup (170 ml), plus
2 tablespoons almond or coconut milk
4 tablespoons cocoa powder
2 tablespoons maple syrup
pinch of salt
(*See image, front*)

1 Pit the dates and soak them in the warm water for 15 minutes. Drain, reserving the soaking water, and add the dates to a blender or food processor along with the soaking water and all the remaining ingredients. Blend until smooth.

2 Pour into ice pop molds and freeze until set.

CALORIES (PER SERVING)	248
PROTEIN	2.9 g
TOTAL FAT	15.8 g
SATURATED FAT	7.3 g
CARBOHYDRATES	29.2 g
DIETARY FIBER	6.5 g
SUGARS	20.2 g
VITAMINS	K

CABBAGE STRUDEL

Serves 12

Inspired by a traditional Hungarian dish, this strudel recipe showcases the versatility of cabbage.

Prep: 20 mins | Cook: 45 mins

3 tablespoons coconut oil, plus ¼ cup (60 ml), melted, for brushing

½ head green or red cabbage, shredded

1 apple, grated

¼ teaspoon salt

⅓ cup (65 g) unrefined cane sugar, plus 5 tablespoons for sprinkling

½ cup (80 g) raisins

4 sheets filo pastry

1 Preheat the oven to 375°F (190°C). Line a baking sheet with parchment paper.

2 In a large saucepan, melt the 3 tablespoons of oil, then add the cabbage and sauté until tender, about 10 minutes. Add the apple, salt, sugar, and raisins and cook for 3 to 4 minutes, until any juices have cooked off. Remove from the heat and cool completely, about 30 minutes.

3 Lay one sheet of filo pastry on the baking sheet. Brush with melted coconut oil and then sprinkle with 1 tablespoon of sugar. Place a second sheet of filo on top, brush with oil and sprinkle with sugar. Repeat with the final two sheets of filo. Spread the cooled filling lengthwise along the top layer of dough. Roll the dough away from you, tucking in the ends and laying it down on the loose end. Brush the top with oil and sprinkle with the remaining sugar.

4 Bake for 30 minutes, until the top is golden brown, then remove from the oven. Allow to cool for 10 minutes before slicing and serving.

CALORIES (PER SERVING)	188
PROTEIN	1.8 g
TOTAL FAT	8.3 g
SATURATED FAT	6.9 g
CARBOHYDRATES	28.8 g
DIETARY FIBER	1.3 g
SUGARS	16.5 g
VITAMINS	B6, C

RHUBARB AND CHARD PIE

 Serves 8–10

This has got to be one of my favorite recipes. It's a great way to keep those red chard stems from going to waste—they look almost indistinguishable from the rhubarb once everything is cooked up. Of course any color chard stem will fit the bill, but the brightness of the red stems is especially gorgeous.

Prep: 20 mins | Cook: 40 mins

⅓ cup (85 ml) coconut oil or (70 g) vegan butter
1 cup (125 g) all-purpose flour
¼ cup (30 g) powdered sugar

FOR THE FILLING
4 cups (400 g) rhubarb, chopped
2 cups (70 g) chard stems, chopped
1 cup (200 g) unrefined cane sugar
3 tablespoons all-purpose flour
1 tablespoon cornstarch

coconut milk ice cream, to serve

1 Preheat the oven to 350°F (180°C).

2 For the shortbread crust, mix together the oil or butter, flour, and sugar with a fork or your fingers. Press into a 9-inch (23-cm) pie dish. Prick a few times with a fork. Bake for 12 minutes, then remove from the oven and allow to cool.

3 For the filling, place the rhubarb, chard stems, and sugar in a saucepan. Cook over a medium heat for 10 minutes, until the fruit has softened but still holds its shape.

4 Remove from the heat and stir in the flour and cornstarch until no lumps remain. Pour into the prepared crust and bake for 20 minutes, until the filling has firmed up. Allow to cool and serve with a generous dollop of coconut milk ice cream.

CALORIES (PER SERVING)	244
PROTEIN	2.6 g
TOTAL FAT	8.3 g
SATURATED FAT	7 g
CARBOHYDRATES	42.2 g
DIETARY FIBER	1.6 g
SUGARS	26.1 g
VITAMINS	C

WINE-POACHED CHAYOTE "PEARS"

 Serves 6 / gluten-free

This dessert will have your whole house smelling wintry and festive. And there's nothing more festive than incorporating cinnamon, cloves, and an entire bottle of red wine into your dessert!

Prep: 5 mins | Cook: 40 mins

3 chayote squash
1 bottle red wine
1¼ cups (250 g) unrefined cane sugar
2 cinnamon sticks
2 cloves
non-dairy vanilla ice cream, to serve

1 Peel the squash. Quarter them lengthwise and remove the avocado-like seed.

2 Combine the wine and sugar in a medium-sized stock pot. Heat over medium-high heat and stir until the sugar dissolves. Add the remaining ingredients, reduce the heat and simmer until the squash pieces are tender, about 30 minutes.

3 Carefully remove the squash with a slotted spoon. Continue simmering the wine until it has reduced down to approximately 1 cup (250 ml) of sweet red wine syrup.

4 To serve, plate the chayote along with a scoop of non-dairy vanilla ice cream and a drizzle of syrup.

CALORIES (PER SERVING)	288
PROTEIN	1 g
TOTAL FAT	0 g
SATURATED FAT	0 g
CARBOHYDRATES	51.8 g
DIETARY FIBER	1.5 g
SUGARS	42.7 g
VITAMINS	C

SAGE AND LAVENDER TEA

Serves 1 / gluten-free

A fresh herbal tea is perfect to drink alongside all of these wonderful cakes. Sage is known for its ability to calm nerves, and lavender for its relaxing qualities: a little cup of heaven is waiting in your garden to be picked.

Prep: 5 mins | Cook: 10 mins

10 fresh sage leaves
1 teaspoon fresh lavender leaves
1½ cups (375 ml) boiling water
agave or maple syrup, to sweeten
(*See image, front*)

1 Place the sage and lavender leaves in a mug and pour the boiling water over them. Cover with a saucer to keep the tea from cooling while it steeps for 10 minutes. If desired, sweeten to taste with agave or maple syrup.

CALORIES (PER SERVING)	69
PROTEIN	1.7 g
TOTAL FAT	2.1 g
SATURATED FAT	1.1 g
CARBOHYDRATES	14.6 g
DIETARY FIBER	6.3 g
SUGARS	3.8 g
VITAMINS	A, B6, C

DANDELION MIMOSAS

Serves 6 / gluten-free

A sweet little tipple to end your meal when there's reason to celebrate, or when you simply don't have room for dessert. These mimosas are especially lovely when garnished with a dandelion flower—though only if they're picked from your own organic garden.

Prep: 5 mins | Cook: 15 mins

½ cup (25 g) dandelion greens
½ cup (100 g) unrefined cane sugar
½ cup (125 ml) water
3 cups (750 ml) grapefruit juice
3 cups (750 ml) sparkling wine
(*See image, opposite, rear*)

1 Chop the greens into 1- to 2-inch (2.5- to 5-cm) pieces and set aside.

2 To make the dandelion-infused simple syrup, combine the sugar and water together in a small saucepan and heat over low-medium heat, stirring until the sugar dissolves. Place the dandelion greens in the pan and submerge them with a spatula. Reduce the heat to low for 10 minutes, stirring occasionally. Remove from the heat, and strain through a sieve into a glass. Cool to room temperature before using.

3 Pour 1 tablespoon of dandelion syrup into each glass. Add ½ cup (125 ml) grapefruit juice and stir gently to combine. Top up with ½ cup (125 ml) sparkling wine and serve. Store any leftover syrup in a covered jar in the fridge, where it will keep for several weeks.

CALORIES (PER SERVING)	151
PROTEIN	0.8 g
TOTAL FAT	0.1 g
SATURATED FAT	0 g
CARBOHYDRATES	27.3 g
DIETARY FIBER	1.4 g
SUGARS	24.7 g
VITAMINS	A, C

INDEX

Many sincere thanks to everyone who worked with me on *Greens 24/7*. To Sarah Bloxham, Sam Kennedy, Lucy Parissi, Sorrel Wood, Kerry Enzor, and the entire team at Quantum, and to Matthew Lore, Anne Rumberger, Sasha Tropp, Sarah Schneider, and Karen Giangreco at The Experiment for your countless hours of work, for believing in me, and making this dream a reality. Special thanks to my editor Rachel Malig for all of your hard work and positive spin on things, and for always making yourself available to answer my constant stream of questions. Jackie Sobon, thank you for your gorgeous photography that brought this book to life and made it a work of art.

To my Mom and Dad, thank you for raising me to love food and for having a sit-down meal together every night growing up. And to my brothers James and Patrick for your support and the shared meals we've prepared together over the years.

To my Sunday dinner testers, Jan and Shirley, thank you for letting me cook for you and for always providing such honest feedback. Sandi Ackroyd, thank you for your support, your motivation, and your friendship. And to my friends and family—thank you for being my cheerleaders through this writing process and always.

To my amazing testers who sweated it out in their kitchens as I honed the recipes: Sara Ray, Laura Thompson, Kelly Henderson, Stephanie McCaslin, Melissa Rosvold, Suzanne Poldon, Heather Tigert, Stephanie Lindsay, Maud Pryor, Kyleigh Rapanos, Sarina Wheeler, Michelle Thiele, Tamara Gagnon, Tara Hamilton, Nichelle Nicholes, Justine Villeneuve, and Mary Ambrosino. You rule. And to the always kind Kristy Turner, thank you for your guidance on the testing process.

Most of all, my sweet boys. Woodrow, thank you for your infectious laughter and for showing me how big I can love. And to Mark, thank you for your love and partnership, your unwavering support, your endless dishwashing, and for telling me that you love my cooking more than anyone else's (and meaning it).